Living in the Spirit

Living in the Spirit

free to be free

George Holmes

*Instead of **addictions, afflictions, bad habits, low self-esteem, insecurities, poverty, and self-doubt**, we can live **happy, content, prosperous, wholesome, and healthy** lives, **free** of drudgery and guilt.*

To order additional copies of this book, contact:
Xlibris Corporation
1-888-795-4274
www.Xlibris.com
Orders@Xlibris.com
56136

Contents

Dedication

I dedicate this book to believers in Jesus the Christ everywhere they exist in the world today and to those who will come to know him through the supernatural power of the Word of God. Those who have the Word of God residing in them (Christ Jesus living within them) have at their disposal the power to overcome every obstacle, break down every barrier, and resist every temptation that would hinder them from living a healthy and prosperous life.

Author's Biography

George Holmes lives with his family in rural Alabama where he serves the local church congregation as a deacon. He is a member of the board of trustees, finance officer, assistant superintendent of the Sunday school and sometimes Sunday school teacher, sometimes bible study teacher, and full time custodian of the church buildings and grounds.

Preface

I thank our Lord and Savior, Jesus Christ, for the renewing of my mind; I thank Jehovah God Almighty for finding me worthy of service in His Kingdom; and I thank the Holy Spirit for patiently guiding me through this journey. I thank you, reader, for opening this book, and I pray that God has led you to do so because herein lies the answer to a special need that you have. If you decide to purchase the book, please know that the financial proceeds from your purchase will benefit God's Kingdom. While on the journey through which God has taken me in preparation for this work, I have learned the true meaning of the expression, "free to be free," or as my great grandmother used to say, "Free indeed."

The author assumes that the reader believes the bible to be the divine word of God. Throughout these pages, I make frequent references to scripture to assure you that the ideas expressed are from God's word. Reading this book will not expose you to any new ideas nor will it introduce you to any new doctrine, but I pray that it will lead you to a new commitment to live the life that God has purposed for you. I pray that God will bless everyone who reads this book with renewed inspiration to use the inner strength and power that comes from belief in Jesus Christ to exercise the liberty that Christ purchased for us through His death on the cross. Those who believe in Jesus are free to be free from all of life's strongholds and free to live abundant lives while remaining sanctified, holy, and completely acceptable in the eyes of God. God saves each of us for God's purpose. I pray that in these words you will gain a new enthusiasm to do what God has saved you to do.

Jesus Christ is the perfect and complete image of God. If we know the Son, we also know the Father. If we believe in His Word, we know exactly what God expects of us. If we trust in Jesus, we can be exactly what God intended for us to be.

When we have Christ living within us, we have liberty as well. We are set free to live the life we choose to live. **Addictions, afflictions, bad habits, low self-esteem, insecurities, poverty, and self-doubt** no longer enslave us, but we are free to be the complete persons that God created us to be.

We can be ***happy, content, and prosperous, while living a wholesome, healthy lifestyle, free of the drudgery and guilt*** that come from chasing after the things of the world.

If you, reader, have never done so before, I encourage you to pray the following prayer right now, in sincerity, from your heart: *"Almighty God, I recognize that I am a sinner. Please forgive me for my sins. I thank you for sending your son, Jesus, who died on the cross to free us from the sins that had us bound and for raising him from the dead so that we too might have eternal life. God, I know that all I am, all I have, and all I ever hope to be belong to you. I know that you created me for your purpose. I yield my will to you now. I commit the rest of my life to living for whatever you have purposed for me. Please, come into my life, take control of my life, and baptize me with your precious Holy Spirit, to live within me forever. Amen."*

I pray you will enjoy the journey as much as I have. Thanks and glory to God, Almighty.

Introduction

The foundation of Christianity is the belief that Jesus Christ of Nazareth is the son of God, or God incarnate (*please see John 1:1-34*), and that he became a man through a virgin birth, lived and taught here on earth in the form a human being, suffered the human experience just as we do, was subjected to human temptations just as we are (*please see Hebrews 2:14-18*), but did not *sin*. He surrendered himself to the authorities, endured ridicule and horrific torture, was hanged on a cross where he shed his *blood* until he died, was buried and on the third day *resurrected* again to eternal life, and he returned to Heaven and now rules with God the Father (*please see 1 Corinthians 15*). Someday he will return to earth and at that time, all the dead in Christ and those yet living who are in Christ will be transformed into eternal bodies and live forever as God originally intended when He placed Adam *in the garden in the east.*

In order to comprehend how belief in Jesus Christ will completely set us free from the bondage of sin and death, it is important for us to understand the relationship between *sin,* the *blood,* and the *resurrection.* The first few pages of this book attempt to establish that relationship.

In addition, it is essential that the Christian understands and recognizes the workings and the power of the Holy Spirit. Therefore, through the help of the Holy Spirit, we also give space, with limitation (since the Holy Spirit cannot be completely explained), to a descriptive narrative concerning the Spirit of God.

Sin

Any failure to obey the laws or divine teachings of God is a sin. We classify *failure to take action in accordance with God's word* as sins of *omission*. Any *act, thought or behavior* that is *in opposition* to the word of God is sin. We call these sins of *commission*. We all are sinners because we all inherited Adam's sinful nature. Figuratively speaking, when through Adam sin was introduced into the world it became part of the human bloodline, or part of our DNA. In order to accept this saying, we have to be completely honest in our assessment of ourselves. Most of us believe that we are "good" people. With careful examination, however, it becomes clear that unless we are able to control them, our thoughts, our motives, and our actions would not be "good." In the absence of a higher moral character, we are without fear or God and without regard for man.

God created Adam and Eve "*in the image of God*" and placed them in a beautiful garden "*in Eden, in the east*" (*see Genesis 2:8*). Sin was unknown and the only restriction God placed on the humans was the prohibition from eating the fruit of the *tree of the knowledge of good and evil*. God said when you eat of it you will surely die. The serpent seduced the woman into doubting that God's word was true and persuaded her to eat of the fruit. She persuaded the man to eat of it also. Then "*their eyes were opened and they realized they were naked and they were ashamed*" (*see Genesis 3:8*). This single act of disobedience committed by the man and woman introduced sin into the world.

Just as Adam was, we too were created "*in the image of God*" with freedom of spirit, ability to reason, to analyze the complexities of life, and to choose our own course of action. Because God created us in His image, He has given us the privilege of fellowship with Him. Even as we know we are dependent on God for our existence, we still yield to the temptation to follow our own selfish desires. We ignore the opportunity He has given us and forfeit the peaceful and abundant life "*in Eden, in the east*" in our effort to live independent of God's control. However, He has said, "If you do as I have instructed, you will live forever; if you are disobedient to my word,

15

you must die." Therefore, we spend much of our lives suffering from guilt and anxiety because of the sentence of death that hangs over us.

The psalmist, when writing *Psalm 14* says that God looks down from Heaven and finds not even one who is without sin. The apostle Paul repeats this same assessment in *Romans 3:9-18*.

It is our human nature to live according to the flesh and to seek after our fleshly desires. In *Romans 7:18-25*, Paul writes that we are rotten through and through as far as our human nature is concerned. We are powerless on our own to free ourselves from the desire to do what is sinful. However, Christ died on the cross and offered His blood as *atonement** for the sins of humankind. Through His death and because of His sacrifice, we may obtain freedom from the bondage of our sinful nature. God has extended the offer of atonement through His Son, Jesus Christ, and it is now up to us, individually, to accept that offer. When we accept Jesus Christ as our Lord and Savior, begin to walk according to the will of God (found in His word), allow ourselves to be guided by the Holy Spirit, we are no longer subject to our fleshly desires but are able to bring our thoughts and thereby bring our physical bodies into submission to our Spirit man. In order to do this, it is critical that we have the same Spirit that is in Christ Jesus living in us.

In Christ Jesus, having His Spirit in us, we are free and empowered by the Holy Spirit to live Godly lives that are more fulfilling, more prosperous, and more rewarding than any life the "world" has to offer. This life is what we refer to as "abundant life." Furthermore—I failed to mention the longevity factor—life in Christ is eternal.

> *Leviticus 17:11-14* . . . . *for the life of any creature is in its blood.*
> *I have given you the blood so you can make atonement for your sins.*
> *It is the blood, representing life, that brings you atonement.*

The Blood of the Covenant

Exodus 24:8 And Moses took the blood and sprinkled it on the people, and said, "Behold the blood of the covenant which the Lord has made with you in accordance with all these words."

A covenant is a solemn agreement that is binding on all parties. It is interesting to note that throughout human history, God always dealt with man by covenant. He dealt with the first humans through an agreement with Adam. If man were obedient to the word of God, he would live forever in the garden and be master over all life. In addition, God made this agreement with him: You may eat freely any fruit in the garden except fruit from the tree of the knowledge of good and evil. If you eat of its fruit, you will surely die.

He dealt with the second humans through an agreement with Noah. He offered man the same opportunity as he had offered Adam—multiply and fill the earth. In addition, he made this agreement with Noah: All of the plants and animals are yours to eat. Do not eat anything that has its blood still in it, and murder is strictly forbidden. For God's part, He said, "Never again will there be a flood to destroy all life. I have set a rainbow in the clouds to remind me of this everlasting covenant."

Then came Abram. Abram believed God, and God declared him righteous because of his faith. God made this agreement with him: Follow me and I will protect you, and your reward will be great. Your descendants will be too numerous to count, and I will give them all the land between Egypt and the Euphrates River. Furthermore, your name shall be Abraham. I will make you the father of many nations. Kings shall be among your descendants. I will be their God. This covenant will continue forever. Circumcise each male among you as a sign that you have accepted this covenant.

After God freed Moses and the Israelites from captivity in Egypt via the miraculous escape through the Red Sea, He gave them His law and His promise of safety and protection from their enemies. The people promised to observe and obey everything written in the Book of the Covenant. Moses took the blood of young bulls, sprinkled it on the altar and on the people, and said, "This blood confirms the covenant the Lord has made with you in giving you these laws." (*Please see Exodus 24:1-8.*) This "blood of the covenant" would become the foundation for all future sacrifices and a symbol of the agreement between God and man.

Moses commanded the people of Israel to sprinkle blood on the doorposts so that the angel of death would not kill their firstborn sons. Even today, the blood of the covenant is so sacred the scriptures warn that punishment awaits those who have treated the blood of the covenant as if it were common and unholy.

God made a promise to King David that He would raise up one of David's sons and establish his kingdom forever. "I will be his father and he will be my son. I will establish him over my dynasty and my kingdom for all time, and his throne will be secure forever."

Enter Jesus Christ of Nazareth centuries later. Christ gives us clues throughout his ministry that his blood is the "blood of the covenant" that is to be the final sacrifice for the sins of humankind. "I tell you the truth," he said symbolically, "unless you eat the flesh of the Son of Man and drink his blood you cannot have eternal life within you." Again he says, "But anyone who eats my flesh and drinks my blood has eternal life, and I will raise that person at the last day. My flesh is true food, and my blood is true drink. Anyone who eats my flesh and drinks my blood remains in me, and I in him."

I believe the "flesh" that Jesus Christ invites us to eat is the Word of God and the "blood" he bids us to drink is our acceptance of his work on cross.

A short time before his death as he is sharing the Passover meal with his disciples Jesus pours a glass of wine and offers it to them saying, "This is my blood, which confirms the new covenant between God and His people. It is poured out as a sacrifice to forgive the sins of many." (*Please see Matthew 26:28.*) Then as he hangs on the cross, one of the soldiers pierced his side with a spear, and immediately blood and water flowed out (*Please see John 19:34*). Among his last words, we hear him say, "It is finished." The work he came to do, the purpose for which he came, is now complete.

In testimony to Christ's sacrifice, Paul writes in his letter to the Romans, "For God presented Jesus as the sacrifice for sin. People are made right with God when they believe that Jesus sacrificed his life, shedding his blood. And since we have been made right in God's sight by the blood of Christ, he will certainly save us from God's condemnation. (*Please see Romans 3:25, 5:9*)"

The writer of Hebrews presents an even more convincing testimony of how God reconciled man to himself through the blood of Christ on the cross. Hebrews tells us that because we are flesh and blood, Christ also became flesh and blood. For only as a human being could he die, and only by dying could he break the power of Satan, who had the power of death. The high priest of the Old Testament had to enter the Most Holy Place once a year and offer the blood of animals for his own sins and for the sins the people. But Christ, with his blood—not the blood of goats and calves—entered the Most Holy Place once for all time and secured our redemption forever. If under the old system, the blood of goats and bulls and the ashes of a young cow could cleanse people's bodies from ceremonial impurity, just think how much more the blood of Christ will purify our consciences from sinful deeds so that we can worship the living God. By the power of the eternal Spirit, Christ offered himself to God as a perfect sacrifice for our sins. And he did not enter heaven to offer himself again and again, like the high priest here on earth that enters the Most Holy Place year after year with the blood of an animal. For it is not possible for the blood of bulls and goats to take away sins. We can boldly enter Heaven's Most Holy Place because of the blood of Jesus. Our guilty consciences have been sprinkled with Christ's blood to make us clean, and our bodies have been washed with pure water. *Now God has brought up his son, Jesus, from the dead and ratified an eternal covenant with his blood.* (Please see I Corinthians 11:17-34)

And this is the testimony of Peter: *God the Father knew and chose us to be His children, and it is His Spirit that makes us holy. We must be holy because He is holy. And we who have obeyed him have been cleansed by the precious blood of Christ, the sinless, spotless Lamb of God.* (Please see I Peter 1:13-22)

And this is the testimony of John: *If we live according to the word of God and have fellowship with God, the blood of Jesus, his Son, cleanses us from all sin. Jesus Christ, the first to rise from the dead, and the ruler of all the kings of the world, has freed us from our sins by shedding his blood for us.* (Please see I John 1:5-8.)

Because our debt to sin (death) was paid by the blood of Christ, we too share a covenant relationship with God. He receives us as sons and daughters, with all the benefits afforded to heirs, and all He asks of us is that we come to Him. God promised by the blood of His only begotten son to give us a new heart and a right spirit. Perhaps through His infinite wisdom God provided a way of atonement for Adam even before the fall.

The Holy Spirit

It is through the Holy Spirit that we receive power, inner strength, confidence, and wisdom to do what God has purposed for us to do. God has given each one of us a role to play in the building of God's Kingdom on the earth. We can experience true happiness and true peace only when we begin to fulfill that role. After we accept the free and unmerited gift of salvation through the blood of God's Son, Jesus Christ and make the sincere commitment to live our lives for God's purpose, He sends the Holy Spirit to live within us. With His Spirit living within us, all things become possible in our lives. From that moment, we begin a new and everlasting journey as a new person.

This is not a book about the Holy Spirit, but it is very important that you know and understand its power to effect change in our lives. The Holy Spirit gives us the power to defeat the forces that come against us. It does not matter if your enemy is chocolate chip cookies or a mass murderer trapped inside you, the Spirit of the Almighty God can free you from that enemy.

To begin to understand the power of God's Spirit, consider the many Old Testament men and women, humans just as we are who performed amazing things under the power of the Spirit of God. There was Noah who prepared an ark that housed his family and creatures of every species on earth through a flood that destroyed every other living thing. There were Abraham and Sarah who received strength to bare a son when they were both in their old age (*Abraham was 100 years old and Sara 90*), and Moses and Joshua whom God used to perform many miracles along the journey from Egyptian captivity to the Promised Land. There were Elijah, Samson, Daniel, Gideon, and David. God used these men and women as testimonies to us to the power that is available to those who trust in Him.

The New Testament gospels tell of an angel of God appearing to Elizabeth and Zechariah with the news they would have a son (John the Baptist). The child will be *filled with* the Holy Spirit even while still in his mother's womb (*Please see Luke 1:15*). Later we learn that Mary the mother of Jesus becomes pregnant *through the power* of the Holy Spirit. When her cousin Elizabeth, who is already pregnant, learns of Mary's pregnancy, the Holy Spirit fills Elizabeth. The Spirit-filled baby leaped inside Elizabeth's womb upon hearing the news of the coming of Mary's baby. When their child is born, the father, Zechariah, is *filled with* the Holy Spirit. Thirty years later, we find John the Baptist preaching that Jesus would baptize believers *in the* Holy Spirit. Jesus comes to John to be baptized by him. When he comes out of the water, the Holy Spirit is *seen and heard* as if it was a dove, lighting upon Jesus, and a voice out of Heaven says, "*This is my dearly beloved son, who brings me great joy.*" Immediately after this, the *Spirit* leads Jesus into the wilderness where Satan tempts him. He returns 40 days later to Galilee *filled with* the Holy Spirit. (*Please see Luke 4:1-14*)

Throughout his ministry on earth, Jesus taught his disciples lessons about what they could expect from the Holy Spirit. In Mark 13:11, Jesus tells the disciples, ". . . *when you are arrested and stand trial, don't worry in advance about what to say. Just say what God tells you at that time, for it is not you who will be speaking, but the Holy Spirit.*" In Luke 11:13 he says that God will give the Holy Spirit to anyone who asks him. Before departing the earth on his return to Heaven, he promised to pray to the Father that He would send back a *comforter*, and *advocate*, and *counselor*, which is the Holy Spirit.

Luke records in Acts 2:1-4, 50 days after Jesus' departure, as the believers assembled together on the day of the Festival of Pentecost, the Holy Spirit came and filled them. He had lived *with* the disciples before but returned to live *within* them on that day and He lives *within* Christians today. Just as the Father promised, the Holy Spirit has given us power from Heaven, power to be witnesses for Christ, power to resist the temptations of Satan, power to overcome obstacles to effective witness and righteous living, and power over the strongholds of sin that once bound us. The Holy Spirit gives birth to our spiritual lives and leads to all truth. He interprets the scriptures for us and teaches us the ways of righteousness. He intercedes for us in prayer when we are unsure how we should pray or for what we should pray. He brings joy and peace to our hearts when our lives are troubled, and He directs our paths when we are unsure or have lost our way. He is a constant companion who will lead and guide us in every single aspect of our lives, if we are willing to give our lives over to Him. The Holy Spirit lives within the Christian, teaches us what is true, and helps us to discern right from wrong, good from evil, the godly from the ungodly. The Spirit helps us to remain in fellowship with Christ. He reminds us of our purpose when we have lost sight of our self-worth. When the Holy Spirit controls our lives, we do and think those things that please God.

The Holy Spirit interprets the scriptures for us and it enables us to worship God. (*Please see Luke 24:45*) It helps us to become true worshipers in spirit and in truth. (*Please see John 4:21-24*) When we are true worshipers, we understand and accept that our lives and our bodies are not our own but they belong to Christ. He purchased them with a price—his life. So we do not defile our bodies; instead we give them to God as a living and holy sacrifice. Instead of doing the things that the people in the world do, we allow God to transform our minds so that we become new persons. It is then that we know the will of God and become willing to do what pleases Him. (*Please see Romans 12:1-2*)

The Holy Spirit leads us to a full acceptance of Jesus Christ as our Lord and Savior. Moreover, once we have accepted Jesus in our lives and committed our lives to doing the will of God, the Holy Spirit becomes a continuous presence in our lives. Sometimes its presence is as a small still voice and sometimes as a mighty rushing wind. Always it is like rivers of living water that flows from the heart of Jesus. (*Please see John 7:38*).

Witness to the Powers
of the Spirit

For many years, I thought of the Holy Spirit only as the small still voice inside that warns, guides, teaches, and comforts us continually throughout our waking moments. Only after I recommitted my life to Christ did I come to know by personal experience the Holy Spirit as an all-powerful member of the Trinity, equal in all ways with God the Father and God the Son. Unlike the human conscience, the Spirit is not a continual small still voice, although it can be, but it can also be a shout. Unlike the conscience, the Holy Spirit does not reside in everyone. The Holy Spirit can and does manifest himself as a physical force. Just as you can hear the wind but you cannot tell where it came from or where it is going, I am convinced there is no way to explain the workings of the Holy Spirit. But I have also come to know the Holy Spirit as a "powerful force."

My wife committed her life to living for Christ some time before I did. She had fellowship with other congregations throughout the area where we live, and had visited a particular church whose worship service she felt I would enjoy. She encouraged me to come with her to attend a revival service there. Except for a few other members of our own church who visited that evening, we did not know the members of the congregation or the pastor. During the praise and worship portion of the service, we were enjoying singing praise songs and "lifting holy hands to heaven." For several years, I had suffered from degenerative joint disease and shoulder impingement syndrome. I could not raise my hands above my head without severe pain in the shoulder joints. I had given up on physical therapy and resolved to live with the daily dose of anti-inflammatory drugs. I was standing there with my hands half raised and the pastor pointed to me and said, "Mister, God said your shoulders are healed. Go ahead and raise your hands." I felt a force that moved me back as if someone shoved me, but very lightly. I raised my hands a little more and she said, "Go ahead and raise them high above your head. God said the pain is gone. You are healed." I did as she commanded and I felt a soothing sensation around the joints in my shoulders. That was several years ago now and I am still lifting holy hands *high above my head.* I can shoot a basketball, throw a bowling ball, swing a baseball bat, swing a golf club, and raise my grandson high over my head. I recall that I first received the diagnosis when my son was about the same age as my grandson is now. I had a habit of lifting him high above my head each day when I came home from work. Of all the activities I had to give up, this was perhaps the most difficult to accept. God gave it back to me.

It was during Megafest 2006 at the World Congress Center in Atlanta, while surrounded by thousands of witnesses from around the country, I witnessed a move of the Holy Spirit that will forever be etched in my mind. It involved a woman who calls herself "prophetess" and one whom it had been difficult for me to listen to before. I thought she was a very emotional person who always spoke with a screaming voice. I have a very hard time following or comprehending the message of people who speak in loud voices. I am not sure if it results from damage to my eardrum received when I was a child or from the constant scolding I received from my mother while growing up. I had always avoided the prophetess. On this day, however, I went with several other members of our congregation, including our pastor, to hear her speak. And on this day, the woman spoke in such a peaceful manner that I found myself hanging on every word. It was as if she was speaking directly to me, so much so that many who were in our group still tease me about the turnaround of my attitude towards her. She talked about the cloud that God used to lead the Israelites after their release from bondage to the Egyptians. She spoke of how God was in the cloud and how He covers us if we would only trust God and believe in His covering. She said that for the thousands of us who had come from small churches all over the country, God would provide us with an experience we could return to our small communities and relate to our brothers and sisters how God is still in the cloud and he still covers us. I heard her say, "Some of you will not feel a thing. Some of you will have to take care of others. Some of you will be swept off your feet by what you are about to experience." She offered a prayer and as she finished praying, she came down from the stage and began walking through the arena. As she walked through the isles, people on each side of the isles fell onto the concrete floor and in between seats as purses, shoes, papers, hats, and jackets flew through the air. I stood alongside my pastor and watched as wave after wave of people fell from a force like a mighty wind. She went up one isle and down another, repeatedly until she had covered the entire arena. By the time she returned to the stage, there were people rolling on the floor of the arena, thousands of people crying, some screaming, some even ran from the arena in apparent fear. People with medical professions, or claiming so, were going around offering to examine those who had "passed out" to see if they suffered any neurological damage. I watched one woman from our party roll over the concrete floor for several minutes. She rolled like a log at incredible speed for a person of her age and physical abilities, and she would stop suddenly and roll in the other direction. I noticed there were many others rolling on the floor in the same manner. Another member of our group just sat for nearly an hour with a big beautiful smile on her face, eyes wide open but seemingly not conscious of our presence. Every few minutes she laughed with a beautiful laughter. We found her shoes, jacket, and purse several rows from where we sat. Later she would say that she saw her entire childhood replayed for her during that hour.

I often ask of God, "Why have you allowed me to have these experiences?" The answer I hear continuously is, "So you can tell others."

Freedom from Condemnation

Romans 8:1-4. So now there is no condemnation for those who belong to Christ Jesus. For the power of the life-giving Spirit has freed you through Christ Jesus from the power of sin that leads to death. The Law of Moses could not save us because of our sinful nature. But God put into effect a different plan to save us. He sent his own Son in a human body like ours, except that ours are sinful. He did this so that the requirement of the law would be fully accomplished for us who no longer follow our sinful nature but instead follow the Spirit.

If we are of Christ, then his Spirit lives within us. His Spirit, the life-giving Spirit, is the Holy Spirit. He was present from the beginning of creation and is the power that accomplishes the rebirth of every Christian. The Holy Spirit gives us the power we need to live a Christian life.

In the first verse of Romans 8, we find the word *condemnation*. It means to be declared guilty, to be set aside for punishment. The scripture tells us that for those who belong to Christ (those who have the Spirit of Christ living in them, those who are obedient to the Word of God, and those who have committed their lives to God) God has declared them NOT guilty. Their punishment has been "set aside." The military Manual for Courts Martial provides that punishment for a particular set of violations of the Uniform Code of Military Justice (UCMJ) may be "set aside" by the courts martial convening authority. When a punishment is set aside, all references to the violation are expunged, or completely removed, from the member's record. You might say that when we accepted Jesus Christ as our Lord and Savior, God expunged our past sinful deeds from our records. Perhaps you are thinking, "Why is it necessary? I live a good life. I treat my fellowman with dignity and respect. I give to the poor. I do not murder, steal or commit adultery. I love my neighbor. I have no need for a pardon."

Consider this. We know that God is holy and God is righteous. He will not have communion with that which is unholy or unrighteous. In order for God to declare us blameless by our own merits, we must be perfect in thought and deed. We must live a life that is completely free of the sins of omission and free of the sins of commission. He who is guilty of breaking one tenet of the law is guilty of violating the whole law. Good works and legal compliance with the law alone cannot restore us to a right relationship with God. We must live according to the principles on which the law is based, and we can do this only through genuine love for and reverence of God who gave us the law. Except to those whom the son has chosen, we cannot know the perfect will of God. No set of written, or spoken, rules is sufficient to guide us into the path of righteousness or keep us within the will of God. However, God places His Spirit within us to provide up-to-the-minute guidance, situation-by-situation, from day to day, because the same situation tomorrow might call for a different reaction than yesterday.

It is therefore necessary that we receive Jesus Christ as our lord and savior, because it is through him and only through him, God declares us righteous in His eyes. God offered his only begotten son as a sacrifice, a sin offering, to free us from condemnation. Christ's blood of atonement makes it possible for us to share a personal relationship with God the Father and thereby receive His life-giving spirit.

Carnal Minded
or Spiritual Minded?

Romans 8:5-8. Those who are dominated by their sinful nature think about sinful things, but those who are controlled by the Holy Spirit think about things that please the Spirit. If your sinful nature controls your mind, there is death. But if the Holy Spirit controls your mind, there is life and peace. For the sinful nature is always hostile to God. It never did obey God's laws, and it never will. That's why those who are still under the control of their sinful nature can never please God.

Accepting Christ does not automatically remove our sinful nature but it enables and empowers us to follow the Spirit. We must examine ourselves to determine if we are controlled by our old sinful nature (carnal minded), or if we are controlled by the Holy Spirit (Spiritual minded). My wife often makes the analogy that we have within us two competing spirits—one good and one evil. She compares these spirits to physical bodies. Our thoughts and actions are physical exercises that build strength and endurance in these bodies. The more exercise the body gets, the stronger it becomes. Since these bodies are in direct competition with each other, the stronger one will suppress the weaker. Therefore, if the evil spirit gets more exercise than the good spirit, it becomes stronger and dominant and it forces the good spirit into submission. When this happens, the evil spirit that is within us controls us.

Those of us who call ourselves Christians, who are committed to our walk with Christ, must ask ourselves the question, "Am I carnal minded or Spiritual minded?" To find the answer to the question, we must take an honest, in-depth look inward at our thoughts and actions and attitudes. Galatians 5:19-23 outline behavior that is characteristic of one who is controlled by his or her sinful nature, or carnal mind.

Galatians 5:19-23: *When you follow the desires of your sinful nature, the results are very clear: sexual immorality, impurity, lustful pleasures, idolatry, sorcery, hostility, quarreling, jealousy, outbursts of anger, selfish ambition, dissension, division, envy, drunkenness, wild parties, and other sins like these. Let me tell you again, as I have before, that anyone living that sort of life will not inherit the Kingdom of God. But the Holy Spirit produces this kind of fruit in our lives: love, joy, peace, patience, kindness, goodness, faithfulness, gentleness, and self-control. There is no law against these things!*

In order to be set free from the chains that bind us, we must first recognize and admit that we are bound. A careful study of the characteristics of one who is a slave to the flesh and an honest evaluation of ourselves will help us to gain the freedom we seek.

- **Sexual immorality** is the first of the outward characteristics of the carnal mind listed in the text. It is exhibited through acts of adultery, fornication, perverse sexual pleasures such as pornography, homosexuality, beastiality, incest, promiscuity, and whoremongering. Because these acts occur in relative privacy, they can develop into lifestyles that allow us to lead double lives as we go on with our daily routines as church and community leaders. We believe our indiscretion is hidden from the world and perhaps subconsciously believe that it is ok with God.

Through personal experience, I learned that pornography is as addictive as any drug. I thought it to be a harmless act that was committed in the privacy of my bedroom. No other person was involved so I could easily hide my secret, even when I lived in the house with others. Pornography can be stowed away in photos on a computer diskette or CD-ROM, or movies on videocassette or DVD, or magazines hidden under the bed. But this developed into a consuming habit that controlled me and took up my time and diverted my attention away from other matters as I found myself seeking more and more porn. I even risked my job to "surf the web" for pornography on the office computer. I did this knowing that it could possibly cost my job, my security clearance, and my entire career. Because the office computer was much faster than my home computer, I would use my breaks or even skip lunch to download porn.

Over time, these pornographic images no longer satisfy and the victim turns to prostitutes or to promiscuous sex partners. In cases where the pornography involves violent or perverse acts, it may even lead to abuse of a spouse or sexual partner.

The scriptures warn that we "must not become a slave to anything." Our bodies were made for the Lord and should not be joined with prostitutes. No other sin so clearly affects the body as sexual immorality. Our bodies are the temples of the Holy Spirit, bought by God with a high price, and so we should honor God with our bodies.

It is very hard to avoid the constant stream of temptations to engage in sexual immorality. The provocation is almost everywhere. God's word warns us not to imitate the people of the world. We are to be in control of our thoughts and of our bodies. Through the words of God from Leviticus, Chapter 18, we learn that if we listen to God, through the Spirit that he has placed in us, we will find life through His words.

His word tells us not to engage in sexual relations with close relatives. This also includes anyone who has had a relationship with father, or mother, or brother, or sister, or uncle, or aunt. Do not engage in sexual relationship with a sister or brother, half-sister, half-brother, or stepbrother or stepsister, whether she or he was born into the same household or some other household. Grandparents are not to have sexual relations with their grandchildren. Do not have sexual relations with a father's sister or your mother's sister.

Do not engage in sexual relations with a daughter-in-law or son-in-law. Do not have sexual relations with both a woman and her daughter or a man and his son. Do not take her granddaughter, whether her son's daughter or her daughter's daughter, and have sexual relations with her. The bible describes these relationships as wicked acts.

While your husband or wife is living, do not have sexual relations with a brother-in-law or sister-in-law. Do not have sexual relations with a woman during her period of menstrual impurity. Do not have sexual intercourse with a neighbor's wife.

Do not practice homosexuality, having sex with another man as with a woman. It is a detestable sin. A man must not defile himself by having sex with an animal. A woman must not offer herself to a male animal to have intercourse with it. This is a perverse act.

The bible offers us good examples of how sexual immorality can lead to ruin. None, in my opinion, is more compelling than the example of King David. While David was a great warrior, a great king, and a man after God's own heart, his sexual indiscretion with Bathsheba, the wife of one of his soldiers, caused God to place a curse on his household. As a result, murder was a constant threat in his family, his household rebelled against him, another man had his wives in public view, and his first child by Bathsheba died. His son of one of his wives raped his daughter of another wife, a son killed another of his sons, and on and on. For God to impose such a penalty on such a man of God as David speaks clearly as to how much God hates the sin of sexual immorality. (Please see 2 Samuel, chapters 12-20)

- **Impure thoughts** are as seeds planted in fertile soil. If we lay awake at night thinking up evil plans, it is likely we will rush in the morning to carry out the wicked schemes that are within our power to do. Our thought-life defiles us. I am convinced that sin is more an attitude than a behavior. Perhaps that is why Christ said anyone who looks at a woman with lust in his eye has already committed adultery with her in his heart. He also said *from the heart come evil thoughts, murder, adultery and all other sexual immorality, theft, lying and slander. All the vile things that come from within are what defile us and make us unacceptable to God. (Please see Matthew 5:28, 15:19, and Mark 7:20-23)* Impure thoughts are destructive because our thoughts are the foundations for our actions. If we entertain the thought long enough, it will eventually become an act. To bring our thought life under submission to the will of God, we must fill our hearts with the word of God. Whatever the heart desires, the mind can rationalize. As a man thinks, so is he. You are what you eat. Good thoughts breed good deeds and evil thoughts feed bad deeds. Evil acts begin with evil desires. The clichés are all true.

We are far better if we do not know some of the information that is made available to us. Therefore, we must train our minds to filter out the garbage. Listening to gossip about another person can adversely affect your relationship with that person. It is sometimes necessary for us to make friends or co-workers aware that we do not want to hear the gossip. If we fill our minds with thoughts that are pure and allow the Spirit of Christ to take control of us, we can resist the temptation to think of ways to indulge our evil desires.

- **Eagerness to satisfy lustful pleasures** will surely lead to destruction. Solomon admonishes us to run away from the object of our lustful desire. Those who have responsibility to supervise members of the opposite gender might easily relate to the example of the attractive subordinate. It is possible to develop a physical attraction to a subordinate that, during a counseling session or while on a business trip together or working on an intense project, could develop into an emotional attraction as well. If lead by our carnal mind, this situation could lead to an unexpected sexual encounter. If we are eager to satisfy our lustful pleasures, we are vulnerable to becoming ensnared by what the scriptures describe as "*the evil seductress whose feet go down to death and whose steps lead straight to the grave.*" (*Please see Proverbs, chapter 5*) When lead by our sinful nature, we become like moths drawn to the fire. The Holy Spirit gives us the power to resist our lustful desires and teaches us ways to fight the temptations to do what is wrong.

- **Idolatry** or anything that takes a higher place in our lives than God will cause us to misplace our focus. The scripture tells us in Exodus 34:14, "*You must worship no other gods, for the Lord, whose very name is Jealous, is a God who is jealous about his relationship with you.*" While we live in a society that is mostly monotheist (believe in one God), we must be very careful that we do not allow some of the many things that clutter our lives to become gods in our lives. If we become too attached to things such as jobs, money, homes, and automobiles, we begin to worship the creations instead of the Creator. Instead of praising God and thanking Him for allowing us to have these things, we begin to see them as "ours" or things we achieved on our own. It may be helpful to see our possessions as Job did and develop the attitude he had when he said, "*The Lord God gives, and the Lord God takes away.*"

Unless we are careful, we may fall victim to the blackjack table, the lottery or stock market, the horse races, the dog track, drugs and alcohol, or even our own bodies. Whatever thing we allow to occupy the highest place in our lives becomes our god.

Hero worship has the potential to ensnare us if we forget that those who teach, those who preach, or minister, even when they exhibit "god-like" character, are but human. As humans, they have within them that sinful nature. A man's thoughts and behaviors may change with the season of his nature. It is possible that the very same person who was instrumental in leading you to seek a relationship with Christ will do or say something that causes you to fall away. For this reason, it is important that we remain focused on and place our trust in God and not in man.

The accumulation of unneeded possessions can become an addiction in our lives. This greed may cause us to commit petty crimes such as shoplifting or stealing from our employers. Greed may cause us to neglect other important areas of our lives or other people in our lives while we work additional jobs and spend all our money on things we falsely believe we need. It is important that we continually direct our focus on God by reminding ourselves that every good and perfect gift comes from Him.

We must remember that we are only visitors here on earth in this life and but for a short time compared to the eternity after this life. The things of this life are all temporary. What does it profit a man to gain all of this world's goods and lose his soul?

- **Demonic activities**, fortune-tellers, devil worshipers, root doctors, and those who claim they are able to communicate with the dead are all in opposition to the word of God. *Some of these will even present themselves as prophets sent from God* (Please see Deuteronomy 18:10-12, 22). The bible warns us to *be sober and vigilant because the devil walks about seeking any of us whom he may devour.* (Please see 1 Peter 5:8) Satan enters into our souls through the gates of our fleshly desires or our carnal minds. These gates are sight, sound, taste, smell, and touch. Little things we do in secret that do not affect another person may provide an entranceway for Satan to gain control of us. Once Satan has invaded us, his influence in our lives produces thoughts and eventually acts of violence, lust, and greed. These are the thoughts that lead to spouse and child abuse, even murder, fornication, adultery, homosexuality, incest, bestiality, and even child molestation.

Just as the children of Israel worshiped Baal, there are those among us who have chosen to worship The Devil, Lucifer, the Anti-God, The Dark Lord or Satan or whatever name they choose to call it. Our government recognizes Satanism as a legitimate religion, and the U.S. Constitution grants it protection. Satan worship activities include nudity, perverted sexual acts, homosexuality, and torture of animals and humans. These rituals attract many of our teenagers. These teens prey upon other teens that have problems with low self-esteem and have difficulty making friends. The ideology of Satanists is to do everything opposite of the concepts of God. Indulging in what makes them feel good is necessary no matter what the consequences are to someone else. If society considers something good, to them it is bad. It is better to do bad things to other people. They commit such abuses as rape, sexual assault and torture, or human/animal sacrifices.

Many other less severe "dark" activities attract our attention and indulgence.

> **Deuteronomy 18:10-12, 22:** *And do not let your people practice fortune-telling, or use sorcery, or interpret omens, or engage in witchcraft, or cast spells, or function as mediums or psychics, or call forth the spirits of the dead. Anyone who does these things is detestable to the Lord. If the prophet speaks in the Lord's name but his prediction does not happen or come true, you will know that the Lord did not give that message.*

> **1 Peter 5:8:** *Stay alert! Watch out for your great enemy, the devil. He prowls around like a roaring lion, looking for someone to devour.*

> **1 Timothy 4:1:** *Now the Holy Spirit tells us clearly that in the last times some will turn away from the true faith; they will follow deceptive spirits and teachings that come from demons.*

Witness to Demonic Activity

On numerous occasions during conversations with my pastor, other pastors, congregation members and even my wife, I heard them claim to have seen "demons" or "demonic spirits" on other members or visitors to our worship services. I usually kept silent during these discussions because I doubted these claims. Just after the day I wrote the preceding paragraph on demonic activities, God suffered me to have an experience that opened my eyes, my spiritual eyes, to the possibility of the truth in their claims.

A member of our congregation asked me on Sunday to locate some material for an upcoming program we were planning. I located it on Monday evening and instead of waiting until Wednesday night when we would meet again at Bible Study, decided to drop the material by the member's home that same evening. I could hear loud voices as I knocked on the front door. There was no immediate answer so I knocked again, but this time louder. Still there was no answer. I could hear clearly now that it was only one voice, and I could understand the words. During more than 20 years in the military, I heard a lot of swearing, and there was a time in my life when I "cussed like a sailor." However, I dare not repeat the profanity that spewed from the lips of the person whose voice I heard through the door. I did not want to hear what I was hearing and did not want to leave after having knocked so loud. When the door opened, a woman with the face of a demon greeted me with a brilliant smile, a warm hug, and a loving voice that said, "You caught me venting." She led me into the kitchen area where three other people, one who was only 10 or 11 years old, all went about their business as if they are simply spending a quiet, relaxing evening at home. One was reading, another doing dishes and another sat quietly in the corner opposite my friend's chair. I stood there feeling as if I were on the set of the movie "The Exorcist."

Days later, it is difficult to comprehend how the words I heard through the door came from the lips of the person with whom I visited inside. The demon I saw behind the smile and through the eyes of the face that greeted me at the door is still vivid in my mind. I pray that through His mercies,

God provides a way of escape from this demon. I am convinced that unless the Holy Spirit fills us, Satan himself will fill us.

I am reminded of these words from **James 3:10-12**.

> *"And so blessing and cursing come pouring out the same mouth. Surely, my brothers and sisters, this is not right! Does a spring of water bubble out with both fresh water and bitter water? Can you pick olives from a fig tree or figs from a grapevine? No, and you can't draw fresh water from a salty pool."*

- **Hostility** is defined as a feeling or attitude of unfriendliness or opposition. Hostility can erode or even destroy the cohesiveness of a body. We have a need to belong to a community, and we draw strength from others with whom we share a common bond. In the community that is the body of Christ, we find support to help us overcome whatever demon is interfering with our ability to live a wholesome, satisfying and productive life. Getting along well with others enable us to take advantage of that support.

We sometimes exhibit our hostile attitudes in rude behavior that is easily apparent to others and therefore set us apart, even in a large group. In church, we will squeeze our bodies onto an already overcrowded pew to avoid sitting next to someone who is not in our "little group." This "little group" syndrome erodes or even destroys cohesiveness in the body. When the body is divided or its members in opposition, the members that are most in need do not get the support needed to help them overcome obstacles hindering a life of freedom.

In the Old Testament book of Nehemiah, we find an example of how Satan can use the person who has a hostile attitude to thwart the work of the church. Nehemiah has a comfortable and very wealthy position with the government of Persia, but God sends him home to Jerusalem. Perhaps it was for this particular purpose that God had carefully prepared Nehemiah. He arrives and finds the city in ruins and people are splintered and unable to get along with each other. The walls that surround and protect the city are in shambles. Nehemiah begins to rally the people together around a project to rebuild the wall and reunite the city. Sanballat, who is full of anger and hostility, opposes the project and begins talking it down to anyone who will listen. Soon Tobiah joins in with Sanballat and adds in the ridicule and negative talking. Not long after that, Geshem also joins these two, and now what you have is a small clique forming. They fabricate a lie to discredit Nehemiah so the people will not want to follow him. They threaten to tell the King that Nehemiah is planning to overthrow the government in an attempt to frighten him into giving up. As is so often the case, this group has nothing to gain by preventing the building of the wall from continuing. Their opposition is not based on the fact they have a better idea, that the work will cost too much, or that the materials are substandard, or on any other reason except hostility.

We sometimes direct the hostility toward a person who has offended us at some point in the past, or one who does not share our same viewpoints, or who does not live in the same neighborhood, or share a family relationship, or who is not of the same race or ethnicity. This hostility breeds contempt that very often leads to serious offenses against others.

- **Quarreling,** or quarrel, is an angry dispute, altercation or disagreement that is marked by a temporary and often permanent break up of friendly relationships. Other terms sometimes used to describe a quarrel include argument, squabble, and dispute, falling out, bicker, wrangle or fight. By whatever name it is called, quarreling is disruptive and contrary to good order. I have personally witnessed members who arrive at a church meeting intent on starting a fight. They can be heard saying things such as, "I am going to give them a piece of my mind" or "I'm going to set them straight." The tone of voice used in these statements let me know right away that it would not be a friendly conversation.

These quarrels are always rooted in the carnal mind. They usually result when one person takes offense to something another person said or did. One person gets a position that the injured person had expected or desired. The arguments are seldom about the root cause of the problem. The person who is angry because he or she did not get a Sunday School teacher position might argue that Worship Services do not get started on time because Sunday School runs over its scheduled time. The person who is living in an adulterous relationship is angry because the Pastor frequently speaks against adultery. The message convicts the injured person, but instead of repenting, he believes the Pastor is picking on him or her. Therefore, he argues that the church should replace the Pastor because he or she is ineffective.

This kind of behavior hinders us from worshiping God. God is not pleased when we act pious but have unforgiven sin in our hearts and are living sinful lifestyles. (Please see Isaiah 58:1-5)

Our behavior influences young children, unsaved persons, and even other Christians who are weak in the faith. Therefore, we must live our lives according to the word of God. When we commit ourselves to being living examples of God's righteousness, He will withhold no good thing from us. We are the light of the world and therefore should *avoid participating in the darkness of wild parties and drunkenness, or in sexual promiscuity and immoral living, or in quarreling and jealousy.* (Please see Romans 13:13)

- **Jealousy** results when we become resentful or envious of someone else's achievements, attainments, successes, or possessions. It also occurs when we become fearful of losing someone's affection. When we are led by our carnal minds, our focus is directed on things we want for ourselves rather than what God wants for us. If it is the big house or car we want and we do not get it, we become resentful of the neighbor who does have it, especially if we feel we are "more righteous" than he is. This feeling of jealousy hinders us from being thankful to God and happy for our neighbor and will eventually erode our relationship with the neighbor and with God. If we desire to be the lead singer in the choir, but someone who is more suited gets the role, we become resentful of that person. This feeling of jealousy can hinder our own effectiveness because we no longer do our best in our backup role. We allow ourselves to become disruptive and eventually our behavior will hurt the choir. The bible makes it very clear that jealousy is of our carnal mind. It tells us plainly that jealousy and selfishness are not God's kind of wisdom but are earthly, unspiritual, and demonic. *Wherever there is jealousy and selfish ambition, there is disorder and evil. (*Please see James 3:15-16*) Resentment weighs us down much like carrying around a heavy weight of stone or sand, and jealousy is more destructive than anger or the waters of a flood. (*Please see Proverbs 27:3-4*)

Trust is an important element to any partnership, and it is essential in a marriage. A marriage partner who is distrustful of the other cannot function properly in his or her role as spouse. When one party in the relationship is suspicious of the other, the relationship suffers for lack of the support, encouragement, and cooperation that is necessary for a good partnership. Jealousy leads to stress that produces adverse affects on our decision-making, our interaction with others, and our health. The bible tells us that *a peaceful heart leads to a healthy body but jealousy is like a cancer in the bones. Resentment destroys the fool, and jealousy kills the simple.* (Please see Job 5:2)

- **Outbursts of anger** are a sure way of demonstrating to the world outside what is going on inside our hearts. The dictionary defines anger as a strong feeling of displeasure and belligerence aroused by a real or supposed wrong. By understanding the definition, we can see that anger can be good or bad. Anger experienced because of an act of wrongdoing helps us to correct that wrong or reduce the chance that it will happen again. On the other hand, anger at something we perceive as wrong can be very dangerous, especially if our supposition is false. If we are lead by the Spirit, our anger is controlled and our judgment is restrained. Those who are lead by the Spirit are *"quick to listen, slow to speak and slow to anger."* (Please see James 1) However, if we are lead by our sinful nature we will allow our anger to control us. This out of control anger is characterized by outbursts of rage, bitterness, harsh words, dirty language, slander, and malicious behavior. The bible warns that we sin when anger controls us, because anger gives a foothold to the devil. (Please see Ephesians 4)

Anger interferes with our worship of God. Because God is righteous and hates sin, He cannot accept our worship if we are harboring sin for which we have not asked His forgiveness. Pent up anger is sin, and the bible commands, *"Don't let the sun go down while you are still angry."* Of course we cannot control the going down of the sun, but we can control our anger.

There are other ways to deal with anger. The bible records two instances of Jesus becoming angry. In the first, he responds with loving admonition and in the second he responds by shedding tears. When Jesus heard his disciples scolding parents for allowing their children to bother him, he saw this as a teaching opportunity. He used the situation to make the point that we all must seek him as little children. When Jesus arrived at the home of his friends Mary and Martha after the death of their brother, Lazarus, he was angry after finding people crying as they surrounded Mary. The bible says Jesus wept. The bible does not say why he was angry, but it shows that Jesus experienced the same emotions of indignation, sorrow, compassion, and frustration that we face. And just as he controlled his emotions, we can learn to control our own by the power of the Holy Spirit. (Please see Mark 10:13-16 and John 11:32-38). If we are lead by our carnal mind, our response to anger will likely be one that only leads to sin. If we are lead by the Spirit of Christ within us, our responses are more likely to be similar to Jesus' responses as recorded by Mark and John.

Mark 10:13-16: *One day some parents brought their children to Jesus so he could touch and bless them. But the disciples scolded the parents for bothering him. When Jesus saw what was happening, he was angry with his disciples. He said to them, "Let the children come to me. Don't stop them! For the Kingdom of God belongs to those who are like these children. I tell you the truth, anyone who doesn't receive the Kingdom of God like a child will never enter it." Then he took the children in his arms and placed his hands on their heads and blessed them.*

John 11:32-38: *When Mary arrived and saw Jesus, she fell at his feet and said, "Lord, if only you had been here, my brother would not have died." When Jesus saw her weeping and saw the other people wailing with her, a deep anger welled up within him, and he was deeply troubled. "Where have you put him?" he asked them. They told him, "Lord, come and see." Then Jesus wept. The people who were standing nearby said, "See how much he loved him!" But some said, "This man healed a blind man. Couldn't he have kept Lazarus from dying?" Jesus was still angry as he arrived at the tomb, a cave with a stone rolled across its entrance.*

James 1:19-21: *Understand this, my dear brothers and sisters: You must all be quick to listen, slow to speak, and slow to get angry. Human anger does not produce the righteousness God desires. So get rid of all the filth and evil in your lives, and humbly accept the word God has planted in your hearts, for it has the power to save your souls.*

Selfish ambition here refers to egotistical goals or self-centered objectives that are not in line with God's purpose for our lives. Any time we endeavor to achieve a desire or dream where we are the sole beneficiaries, there is danger of being outside the will of God. James 3:16 also tells us that *wherever there is jealousy and selfish ambitions, there is disorder and every evil thing.* Although God has the power to cause our selfish actions to work out for the benefit of His purpose, He will judge the intent in our hearts. Take the choir member who feels he should be the leader of the youth choir as an example. The thought of being out in front and in charge thrills him. He continually sows seeds of discord by pointing out every single error or perceived shortcoming of the current choir leader. At the same time, he works very hard at learning new songs and at discovering who in the choir has the vocal ranges for the various styles. He cannot wait for the opportunity to show the congregation that he is better than the choir leader. While his motives are strictly selfish and his heart is spewing out venom directed at the choir leader, God is preparing him for something good in the future. However, before God can use this choir member for the purpose for which He has planned, God will have to judge his evil heart. Jesus taught his disciples, and us, that if we want to be a follower of Christ, we must turn from our selfish ways, take up our cross, and follow him. We all have ambitions and these are usually healthy for us; however, we must be willing in our hearts to submit ourselves to God's purpose in our lives.

- **Division** in any group will most often weaken that group. "Divide and conquer" is a tactic that has defeated opposing forces throughout history. In the book *The Bait of Satan* the author, John Bevere, describes how Satan uses "offense" to create division among Christians. The author describes offense as one of Satan's most deceptive snares used to pull believers out of God's will. Jesus said, "*It is impossible that offenses will not come . . .*" (Luke 17:1). Nevertheless, we are often unaware when the bait of Satan has ensnared us. Offenses will come, and it is up to us how we let them affect our relationship with God and others. We become offended (our feelings are hurt) very easily when our primary focus is on our own ambitions or ourselves rather than what is best for the group. Each time something does not go our way or something is said that opposes our viewpoint, we are hurt. These hurt feelings lead to disagreement or strong differences of opinion and ultimately a split in the group. We gravitate toward smaller groups or little cliques where we can find someone who agrees with us. The result is several small cells in the church where members will only support those programs or activities where someone in their own group is the sponsor. Church congregations often split when one of these smaller groups decides to move to another church body or even form one of its own. If we are obedient to the word of God, always esteeming others higher than ourselves, we will develop the kind of love and respect for others that lead us to be mutually supportive instead of divisive.

- **Feeling that everyone else is wrong except those in our own little group** is a very unhealthy attitude. Different does not equal wrong. Just because I despise the person who said it does not make it wrong.

We sometimes remove ourselves from the position in which God has placed us because of disagreement with someone in that place. We miss important messages because the message is not in line with our thinking and therefore must be wrong. We fail to grow because we are unwilling to open our hearts and minds to accept the fact we do not know everything and others might have something of benefit to offer us. We impede the progress of the church body by insisting that everything be done our way and by neglecting the ideas and opinions of others and by withdrawing our support from the initiatives of others except those in our little group. We become prisoners to our own faulty attitudes.

- **Envy** is the resentful or unhappy feeling of wanting somebody else's success, good fortune, qualities, or possessions. Jealousy, greed, covetousness, resentment, or grudge is often the outward characterization of envy. Wanting what somebody else has will make us adulterers, even if not in the physical sense, it causes us to commit adultery in our hearts. Jesus teaches that (Please see Mark 7:20-22) it is what comes from inside that defiles us. *From inside our hearts come evil thoughts, sexual immorality, theft, murder, adultery, greed, wickedness, deceit, lustful desires, envy, slander, pride and foolishness. And these are the vile things that come from within that defile us.* The bible also says (Please see James 4:1-6) *the evil desires at war within us cause us to quarrel and fight because we want what we don't have and so we scheme and kill to get it.* We are jealous of what others have and cannot get it, so we wage war and fight to take it away. God does not give us what we ask because our motives are wrong—we want only to satisfy our own pleasures. The bible says we are adulterers when we do this. We are in love with the things of the world. When we fall in love with the things of the world, we become friends with the world. If we become friends with the world, we make ourselves enemies of God.

- **Drunkenness** is to become delirious, impaired, or intoxicated because of having consumed too much alcohol or other intoxicating drug in too short a period. Drunkenness robs us of our effectiveness as Christians. Nothing good ever results from drunkenness, at least not for the one who is drunk. Throughout the bible, there are references to persons being made drunk so another person could take advantage of them. The word drunk is also used to describe someone who is not thinking clearly or who is out of his mind or is unable to walk without staggering.

Recall witnessing how someone you knew became drunk and did or said something that was uncharacteristic of that person, even something for which they, and we, were afterward ashamed. When I was young, I believed drinking made me appear adult or cool. Some older people get drunk to escape reality; some get drunk for fun; and others want to forget their problems or circumstances. In reality, getting drunk does not solve problems; it deepens depression instead of eliminating it; and it destroys our bodies. Drunkenness impairs our ability to think rationally. In the home, it leads to name calling, arguments and fights, child and spouse abuse and neglect. It has too often resulted in murder or the accidental death of a loved one. It can be financially devastating in the home when the person afflicted by this sinful habit of the flesh is the one who controls the family's finances. Drunkenness is not of the Spirit but of the flesh. Drinking alcohol is not cool. If we can persuade young people to learn of Christ and accept him into their lives at an early age, before they have experimented with alcohol, perhaps millions of cases of alcoholism could be avoided.

Christ saved us to be witnesses in God's Kingdom. We cannot be effective witnesses if we have lost our credibility. God charges us to be blameless before the world, but how can we unless we remain sober at all times. How can we be effective soldiers in God's army unless we are prepared to do battle—on a moment's notice? When God needs a soldier for a mission, will He have to wait until we recover from being drunk or "hung over?"

The bible has this to say about the fate of the drunkard: "*Those who indulge in sexual sin, or who worship idols, or commit adultery, or are male prostitutes, or practice homosexuality, or are thieves, or greedy people, or drunkards, or are abusive, or cheat people—none of these will inherit the Kingdom of God.*" (Please see 1 Corinthians 6:9-10)

Witness to Drunkenness

In the rural east Alabama community where I grew up, half of all the people and 90 percent of the men I knew regularly drank alcohol until they were drunk. We lived inside a small circle that consisted of the local church, the school, work (on the farm, sawmill or cotton mill), and the local juke joint. At the local juke joint, there was a party on Friday night and a baseball game on Saturday and therewith two opportunities to get drunk. The baseball games drew many people from miles around to the juke joint and the owner made money selling whatever the people had money to buy, but primarily alcohol. The owner of the juke joint owned the baseball park (pasture), the equipment, and the team. He offered a chance for every young man to play, if he were good enough. And if he were good enough, there was a chance for a young man to become a star in the eyes of all the young ladies, and old men, who came to watch. The pay was usually a case of beer to the losing team and two cases of beer to the winning team and occasionally a jug of "moonshine." I was a baseball star. I graduated from baseball and the cotton mill in rural Alabama and Falstaff and Pabst Blue Ribbon and "moonshine." I advanced to softball and the paper mill in Atlanta and Budweiser and Canadian Mist. Eventually I would go on to become connoisseur of the world's finest beer, wine, and whiskey as I traveled throughout the United States, Europe and Asia. I got drunk with the best of them and in some of the world's best places to get drunk. I spent a lot of money, visited many places, and met many people, and I have nothing to show for it, not even the memories. Being drunk took away my memory. It dulled my senses. While under its influence, I did many things I regret. I made a fool of myself in front of important people. I missed opportunities to influence young people's lives by sharing my experiences, because drunkenness took away my credibility. People do not listen to or believe in a person whom they know to be a drunkard. Had it not been for God's grace and mercy, I might have died and gone to hell while drunk. I was arrested and jailed for reckless driving while under the influence of alcohol. I suffered severe financial and professional penalties for my indiscretion, but the lesson opened my eyes. While attending the mandatory drug and alcohol abuse education and counseling, I saw for the first time how wretched my life had become.

Proverbs 23

Who has anguish? Who has sorrow?
Who is always fighting? Who is always complaining?
Who has unnecessary bruises? Who has bloodshot eyes?
It is the one who spends long hours in the taverns, trying out new drinks.
Don't gaze at the wine, seeing how red it is, how it sparkles in the cup, how smoothly it goes down.
For in the end it bites like a poisonous snake; it stings like a viper.
You will see hallucinations, and you will say crazy things.
You will stagger like a sailor tossed at sea, clinging to a swaying mast.
And you will say, "They hit me, but I didn't feel it.
I didn't even know it when they beat me up.
When will I wake up so I can look for another drink?"

Wild parties: Recalling from the days when I was still "of the world" I attended some awesome parties. My friends and I lived only for the weekend. On some of these weekends, a group of us would pool our money, rent a hotel suite, buy whiskey and food (in that order), and from Friday evening until Sunday night, 6 or 8 or 10 of us, male and female and other, cohabitated within the confines of that small space. Free-flowing alcohol, drugs and sex were the characteristics of our parties. The drugs and alcohol caused us to lose our restraint and our sense of decency to the point that almost anything was ok for us to do. We would spend the entire weekend indulging in revelry and drunkenness, lewd and lascivious behavior, and all kinds of sexual immorality. Occasionally there would be fights between competing suitors. On Monday morning or the next time we met, I could barely look the others in the face because of the guilt or shame. Nevertheless, we repeated this same scene over and over week after week. Participating in this kind of activity destroys our credibility by calling our character into question. The bible says we must separate ourselves from this kind of behavior. It also says our bodies are the temples of the Holy Spirit who lives in us, who is from God, and are not our own. We must take care not to defile the temple.

> **Galatians 5:21b:** *"Let me tell you again, as I have before, that anyone living that sort of life will not inherit the Kingdom of God."*

But there is a more excellent way . . .

Galatians 5:22. *But the **Holy Spirit** produces this kind of fruit in our lives: love, joy, peace, patience, kindness, goodness, faithfulness,*

When we have accepted Jesus Christ as our Lord and Savior and made an earnest commitment to live our lives according to the purpose God has for us, the Holy Spirit comes to dwell within us and in so doing, replaces our selfish desires or our carnal mind with the fruits of the spirit. Only the Spirit can produce these fruits in our lives. We cannot change ourselves by ourselves. This is not intended to imply that these changes will occur in us without some effort from us. In fact, it takes a great deal of effort from us, primarily a sincere willingness and sincere desire to be led by the Spirit. It takes humbling ourselves before God and admitting that we need His help, admitting that we have sinned, with a repentant heart, and making every effort that is within our power to turn from our evil ways. After we have invited Christ in our lives, committed ourselves to living according to the will of God, and God has cleansed us from our old sinful existence, He will fill our lives with the righteousness of God. Christ said that when the evil one returns and finds his house has been swept clean and is empty, he goes out and finds himself seven more demons as evil as himself and they all come to reside there. Therefore, when the house has been swept clean, we must pray for God to fill us with His Spirit. When the Holy Spirit has filled us, he will produce in us love, joy, peace, patience, goodness, and faithfulness.

If we carefully examine our thoughts, attitudes and actions, we can determine if we truly have God's spirit living within us. The bible says anyone who says he loves God but hates his brother is a liar and truth is not found in him. If we love God, we must also love the Son whom He sent. If we love the Son, we will keep his commandments. If we keep his commandments, we need only to ask for whatever we will and he will give it to us, including his Holy Spirit.

Love

It is significant that love is the first fruit mentioned as the fruit of the spirit that the Holy Spirit produces. "Love covers a multitude of sins" is an expression that "church folks" used repeatedly. When I hear this verse from 1 Peter 4:8 quoted and based on the context in which it is used, I often wonder if the speaker has actually read that passage of scripture. It is my belief that God intended for us to understand that if we truly love each other, we will forgive the sins of others, that we will forget their offenses, and that we will not hold grudges against those we feel have mistreated us. Proverbs 10:12 says, ". . . *love makes up for all offenses.*"

It is so important that we love each other that Christ compared it to the way we should love God. In Matthew 22:37-39 he tells us "*to love God with all our heart, soul and mind is the first and greatest commandment and that to love our neighbor as ourselves is equally important.*" Christ taught that we should love not only our neighbor but also our enemies. He taught that we should *do good for those who hate us and pray for those who persecute us* (Please see Matthew 5:43-44). These are the same commandments God gave to Moses and the children of Israel (*Please see Deuteronomy 6:4-5 and Leviticus 19:18*). God's law has not changed.

Jesus also taught us that to love each other is worth more in God's eyes than offerings and sacrifices. Even if we tithe of everything we have, sorrow awaits us if we ignore love and justice for others. It is more important that we love each other than it is to observe our religious practices. He commands us to love each other the same as he loved us. He is our example of how we should love one another. No greater love has one for another than that he should lay down his life for him. Jesus laid down his life for us. Our love for each other shows him that we are his followers.

Because God loves us, he has given us the Holy Spirit to fill our hearts with his love. He expects that we will share that love with each other. Just as God's love is immovable, ours should be also. Just as nothing can ever separate us from God's love, not death nor life, neither angels nor demons, neither our fears for today nor our worries about tomorrow—not even the powers of hell, God expects that nothing will separate us from our love for one another. *No power in the sky above or in the earth below—indeed, nothing in all creation will ever be able to separate us from the love of God that is revealed in Christ Jesus our Lord.* (Please see Romans, chapter 8)

We should not just pretend to love others. We must learn to show that we really love them. If we love each other with a genuine affection, we will take delight in honoring each other. To honor another requires a humble attitude, an attitude that permits us to esteem others higher than ourselves. We encourage others, building them up instead of tearing them down. We celebrate their accomplishments and grieve with them in their times of trouble. We must pray for others, not just generally—God bless our church family—but specifically. The very person or situation we are tempted to gossip to others about is also an opportunity for us to pray to God for that person or situation.

Love owes nothing to anyone—except for our obligation to love one another. If you love your neighbor, you will fulfill the requirements of God's law. Love does no wrong to others. If another believer is distressed by what you eat and you love that believer, do not eat it. Love strengthens the church. Christians should always greet each other with love.

"If I could speak all the languages of the world and the languages of angels, and had the gift of prophecy, and if I understood all of God's secret plans and possessed all knowledge and had the kind of faith that could move mountains and did not love my brothers and sister, I am but a noisy gong or a clanging cymbal, and I would be nothing in the eyes of God. If I gave everything I have to the poor and even sacrificed my body, I would still be nothing if I didn't love my brothers and sisters." Those are the words of Paul, writing to the Corinthians. He also says that love is patient and kind. Love is not jealous, boastful, or proud. Love never gives up, never loses faith, is always hopeful, and endures through every circumstance. Love lasts forever.

We must pray that all the members of our church, community and nation will experience the love of Christ and that we all will be made complete with all the fullness of life and the power that comes from God. We should humble ourselves, be gentle with each other and make allowance for each other's faults. If we do this, we all become more and more like Christ. *He makes the whole body fit together perfectly, each part doing its own special work, helping others to grow, so that the whole body is healthy and growing together and full of love.* (Please see Ephesians 4) It is love that binds us all together in perfect harmony.

As children of the Most High God, we must prove ourselves by our purity, our understanding, our patience, our kindness, by the Holy Spirit within us, and by our sincere love. If we allow ourselves to become lovers of our money and ourselves only, then we will also become boastful and proud, scoff at God, be disobedient to our parents, be ungrateful, and lose our respect for that which is sacred. This kind of attitude produces generational curses in that it produces children who grow up with this same attitude and they pass this attitude along to their children. Therefore, we must set good examples of Christian love for our children. Teach them not to love the pleasures of life more than God. We must constantly encourage others and think of ways to motivate each other to perform acts of love and good works.

When we truly love others and ourselves, it empowers us to restrain from destructive practices. Our focus shifts from self only to doing what is good for others and consequently best for all.

Joy

Joy defined is an emotion of great delight or happiness, a glad feeling, or it is the source or cause for keen pleasure or delight. However, there are two kinds of joy—inward joy that comes from knowing and trusting God and happiness that comes because of pleasant circumstances. Inward joy is steady as long as we trust God; happiness is unpredictable. Inward joy defeats discouragement; happiness covers it up. Inward joy is lasting; happiness is temporary. *"You have given me greater joy than those who have abundant harvests of grain and wine."* (Please see Psalm 4:7)

Joy is so much deeper than happiness. We can feel joy in spite of our deepest troubles. Happiness is temporary because it is based on external circumstances. Joy is lasting because it is based on God's presence within us. We are content when we are able to feel God's presence in our lives day by day. No matter how bad our circumstances get, we have peace as long as we can see God's hand move. And as we learn to trust God more and understand that He works all things together for the good of those who love him and who live according to His purpose, we experience true joy. *"No wonder my heart is filled with joy, and my mouth shouts his praises! My body rests in safety."* (Please see Psalm 16:9)

The bible teaches us to rejoice when we are persecuted for our faith. Why would anyone find joy in persecution? Although we might suffer from persecution, we have faith that God will not allow us to perish but will bring us safely through it. Persecution takes our eyes off earthly rewards. It breaks down our superficial beliefs and helps us understand why it is not good to place our faith in man but God. It strengthens the faith of those who endure and hold out until the end. And by keeping a positive attitude as we go through, it serves as an example for others who will follow. Therefore, the joy comes from knowing going in that we will be better and stronger as we emerge on the other side of our situation. *"God blesses you when you are mocked and persecuted and lied about because you are my followers."* (Please see Matthew 5:11)

The same faith that enables us to endure persecution will also enable us to suffer loss of loved ones, disappointing relationships, loss of finances, and breaking of bad habits or addictions.

True joy helps us to rise above our circumstances. It comes from having a consistent relationship with Jesus Christ. We know that God loves His son and that Jesus loves us. When we are obedient to Christ, we remain in his love, just as Jesus obeys God and remains in God's love. And when our lives are interweaved this way, he will help us to walk through adversity without sinking into the lows that trap us and stop us dead in our tracks and keep us from moving beyond those things that bound us. He will help us to manage prosperity without moving into deceptive highs that cause us to forget who the true source of our blessings is. The joy of living in Christ will keep us grounded securely and levelheaded, regardless of how high or how low our circumstances. The key to immeasurable joy is living in intimate contact with Christ, who is the source of all joy. When we do, we will experience God's special care and protection and see the victory God brings even when defeat seems certain.

Joy can help us to overcome jealousy. When we learn that God has singled someone else out for a special blessing, instead of greeting the news with envy we should rejoice in our heart. We must understand and accept that God uses his people according to his purpose.

When we discover that God is the source of our strength and learn to trust that He will deliver us from whatever temptations we face and learn to trust him with all our hearts, He helps us. When we understand this, our hearts are filled with joy.

The bible says the angels in heaven rejoice when an unbeliever repents and turns to God. This should be our attitude toward sinners and believers who have fallen away when they repent. We must accept them wholeheartedly; welcome them, support, and encourage them so we can help them to grow in Christ. If God has forgiven them for the wrong things they have done, we too should be able to forgive them, be happy for them and move forward. Our hearts are filled with joy from knowing that we always deal justly with others and that we always do what is right.

We get joy from knowing that Jesus has found us worthy of a visit. "Zacchaeus quickly climbed down and took Jesus to his house in great excitement and joy." Zacchaeus was a hated tax collector. He, like other tax collectors of the Roman Empire, had been born a Jew. He chose to work for the Roman government as a tax collector. Tax collectors of that era were notorious for cheating the Jewish people by overcharging them and keeping the money for themselves. Despite the fact, others saw him as a traitor and a robber, Jesus loved him. After he had climbed a sycamore tree to get a look at Jesus, Jesus responded by calling him by name, *"Zacchaeus! Quick, come down! I must be a guest in you home today."* *If we truly seek Jesus he will come into our home and fill our hearts with joy.* (Please see Luke 19:1-10)

Some habits are very hard to break. In the case of drugs or alcohol, our bodies may experience physical anxiety as it learns to function without them. Going through the pains of withdrawal is tough but it cannot compare with the joy that comes from the freedom that is experienced afterward. *It will be like a woman suffering the pains of labor. When her child is born, her anguish gives way to joy because she has brought a new baby into the world.* (Please see John 16:21)

Breaking the Chains that Had Me Bound

When we realize we have been delivered from the thing that had us bound, Joy fills our hearts. This joy comes from knowing that, through the precious blood of His son Jesus, God has set us free from that bondage. We are then able to live our lives openly without fear of retribution or shame. Joy comes from knowing that we have a place of refuge and that place is in the perfect safety of God's grace. When we know God has forgiven us for past indiscretions we can openly confess them and talk to others about them and we have no fear of returning to them. God not only gives us salvation but also He frees us from all unrighteousness.

Military drill sergeants made us experience the joy of overcoming seemingly impossible obstacles. I will never forget the feeling of accomplishment that comes after completing a 25-mile road march while carrying a heavy backpack. It is the same after firing three successive rounds from a rifle into a target 50 meters away and having all three rounds strike in a bull's eye the size of a dime. I recall the feeling of joy that came over me after watching my wife give birth to our daughter, then that same feeling again after the birth of our son. But these cannot compare with the joy I feel when I think of how Jesus rescued me from all the things that once controlled me. I was once slave to drugs and alcohol, pornography and fornication, and more recently tobacco. As God freed me from these addictions, I began to see how all my life I had be slave to something. During my earlier years, it had been clothes, cars, women and drugs. Through the grace and mercy of God, He gave me a wife to rescue me from those things, but I held onto the alcohol and tobacco. A very good friend (I did not know how good a friend he was at the time.) encouraged me to seek God for deliverance. One day as I stood in the "smoking area" outside the building where we worked, he walked by and handed me a small piece of paper. He did not say a word but held out the paper, I took it and he continued on his way. I looked at it and it had these words written on it: "Romans 12:1-2." Later that day I opened the bible to the reference and read these words:

> *"And so, dear brothers and sisters, I plead with you to give your bodies to God. Let them be a living and holy sacrifice—the kind he will accept. When you think of what he has done for you, is this too much to ask? Don't copy the behavior and customs of this world, but let God transform you into a new person by changing the way you think. Then you will know what God wants you to do and you will know how good and pleasing and perfect his will really is." Romans 12:1-2*

I had quit drinking some time before. I had also "*quit*" smoking several times before. I quit drinking whiskey and drank only beer or wine. I quit smoking cigarettes and smoked only a pipe. I quit smoking the pipe and smoked only cigars. I quit for three weeks or I quit for three months. I rationalized that it cannot be bad for me because I am in perfect health. I can run faster and longer than most men half my age. I can drink and not get drunk. They were all lies. Whatever the mind can conceive the heart will rationalize. There must be a renewing of the mind. Each time *I quit*, it was for reasons that were as selfish as the reasons I was smoking and drinking in the first place. How I grew stuck on this notion that "I" could do anything on my own is beyond my comprehension today. I had long before understood that "I" was powerless to change myself and asked God to take control of my life and change me. He had begun a work in me that would change me forever, but it was "He" at work in my life and not "I".

After understanding Romans 12:1-2, I was determined to quit for God and quit for good. I began to realize that as others observed my behavior they might draw an inference that the very thing they see me do is ok to do because I do it. Because I was active in the church and school and in the community, there was much opportunity for others to observe my behavior. I understood that in order to be a witness for Christ, I needed to become more Christ-like.

I have heard others say, "I decided to quit smoking one day. I never picked up another cigarette and I don't even think about them." I wish I knew that secret. I would gladly give it to the world. Quitting was not that easy for me. The power of the Holy Spirit and him only freed me from my addictions. My journey has taken several years and God is not done with me yet.

My attitude toward the use of alcohol and tobacco was this: it is okay to drink or smoke as long as you do it in moderation and as long as you maintain control of it and not allow it to take control of you. In those days, I was unaware of how subtle a seemingly harmless thing can creep in and take control of one's life. After I repented and admitted to God that I was wretched and needed His help to fix me because I could not do it myself, I began to see how my habits were controlling my life. My commute to and from work each day covers approximately 80 miles. I had added another five miles to the trip by altering my route to take me by the gas station each morning to get that first cigar. I got up earlier and instead of making breakfast or spending time with the family, I rushed out each day to feed my craving for nicotine. There were times when I drove to work in the rain or in extreme cold weather with the window open as I puffed on a cigar. I actually believed that it would keep me from smelling like cigar smoke when I arrived at the office. If we went to lunch as a group, I would leave early in order to have a cigar before arriving back in the office. Everyone knew my routine. On the evening drive home, I would make that stop at the gas station to pick up that cigar for after dinner. If you are wondering why I did not buy a box of cigars and save some time, it was the method I devised to limit myself to three per day instead of one every hour. After dinner, I was in the yard, constantly doing yard work but in reality getting that last smoke for the day. Not all of my days went as smooth as this. Sometimes I could not resist the urge to go out in midmorning or at midnight for a cigar. On weekends when I did not have to work, I made up reasons to go to the store.

The Holy Spirit helps us to see things more clearly. I almost never ride in the back seat of our car because whenever I go places with the family, I drive. For years, I believed that if I smoked while driving and my window was open, the smoke should not bother those who sat in the back seat. Soon after I made the commitment to quit, I had the opportunity to ride in the back seat of an automobile while the driver smoked, with the driver's window open, and I almost choked to death. I thought of all the years of hauling my children over thousands of miles in the U.S. and in Europe I have subjected them to inhaling second hand cigarette and cigar smoke. That thought made me feel sick. If you smoke while driving and you want to know how it affects others, try riding in the back seat of an automobile while the driver smokes.

The Holy Spirit helps us in so many ways. The early days of withdrawal were extremely difficult. Because I had been a slave to my habits for so long,

I not only did not know how to break away but also I did not know how bound up I was. I would get dressed and rush out of the house to drive past the gas station in the morning while praying to God along the way to give me the strength to keep going and not stop. It would be days before I heard the Spirit of God telling me it was not necessary for me to drive in that direction to get to work. That is when I began to take the shorter route. Still there are other stores along my way, four of them to be exact. I would have to pray each day to get past those as well. But God always allowed something to distract me or otherwise take away my attention at just the right time. Soon, without realizing I had passed all the stores, I would be at the office—without a cigar. I developed a prayer to get me through lunch and another prayer to get me through dinner. On Saturdays, I often worked from sunrise until sundown or went out with the family. Sundays were not as bad since I had long ago placed tough limits on smoking or drinking alcohol on Sunday (That was part of the plan for self-righteousness I developed before I came into the true knowledge of Salvation.). Breaking the stronghold of alcohol was not as intense as tobacco but it was not without its struggles as well.

I was an ordained deacon by the time I gave up alcohol for good. I had gone "undercover" much earlier but on occasion would find myself open to the world. One day after the funeral of a relative and among the large group that gathers at funerals, I was with old friends with whom I had grown up and they were all drinking. We were at the home of another deacon and he continuously encouraged me, "Have a drink. All of us here are saved and the young folks are all in the backyard." Finally, I gave in and accepted a drink. As soon as I raised the glass to my mouth, a hush came over the crowd that sent conviction through my soul. It was as if those who stood around were saying, "We are disappointed in you." Suddenly, as I stood there with the drink in my hand, it appeared to me that young people began coming from everywhere. That was not only my last public drink, but that was my last drink. For a long time after, there were times when I wanted a beer so badly I could taste it. But I resolved to myself that I would not take a drink in response to that urging. When I do take another drink, it will not be because I felt compelled to do so. I am not implying that any other person should not take a drink if he or she feels that is ok for them. God has told me not to drink—or smoke—so I will not.

I am convinced that when the Holy Spirit does a cleansing, it does a thorough cleansing. Not only did it free me from the strongholds of alcohol and tobacco but also from soft drinks and ice cream and candy. I do not say

I no longer eat these things. I do on occasion. However, I now understand the subtleties of control. Whenever I feel I must have it, this is the time when I must refuse it. I am fully aware that Satan has many schemes and, therefore, I continually pray for God to give me the wisdom to discern the tricks and the strength to resist. *"Oh, what joy for those whose disobedience is forgiven, whose sins are put out of sight."* (Please see Romans 4:7)

Therefore, since we have been made right in God's sight by faith, we have peace with God because of what Jesus Christ our Lord has done for us. (Please see Romans 5:1)

Peace

. . . free of discord; a calm repose; free of strife; harmony in personal relationship, especially with God

True peace comes from knowing God has forgiven our sins. From the physical or carnal perspective, first we want to know that our basic needs are met. For this reason, we pay our mortgage, insurance, utilities, car payment and groceries before the telephone, cable, Internet, health spa, golf club, etc. (Hopefully this all comes after we pay our tithes to the local church.) In the spiritual sense, the Christian knows that we are all born under the penalty of death because of the sinful nature of humankind. We are powerless within ourselves to break free from the hold that sin has on us. But God through His eternal vision gave His son, Jesus Christ, as a sacrifice for our sins, even before we were born. He also promised that if we believe in Jesus Christ, if we trust in his plan for our lives, confess with our mouth that he is our Lord, believing in our heart that God raised him from the dead, we will be saved. When we accept Jesus Christ as Lord of our lives and commit to live according to his plan, which is in obedience to the word of God, the bible, we have forgiveness for our sins through him. While we cannot expect to go through life without ever committing another sin, it is our earnest desire that we do not sin. Consequently, we need only repent in our heart and ask God to forgive us and He has promised to do so. Whatever God said, *is*. Therefore, the basic need for the believer is to have his sins forgiven. When we know that God has forgiven our sins, everything else is secondary. God's forgiveness is everlasting. Once we have become one with Christ, sons and daughters of God, we have eternal life and we have it more abundantly. When troubles come, we will not fear because God is our protector. When sickness or diseases come, we know that God is a healer and a restorer of life. We also know that if we must leave our old bodies and this world, just as God resurrected Jesus from the dead, He will resurrect us as well and will give us eternal bodies in an eternal world. We have peace because we know that God will not leave us alone to suffer through any affliction or addiction but is always there to help us through.

There is peace in trusting God and focusing on his promises for our lives. In order to know the promises God has given us, we must study His word, the bible. Worry, fear, or doubt can rob us of the peace. However, peace is ours if we know what God has said He will do and if we believe that He cannot lie and will do what He said. If we understand that our time is not always His time, and if we trust that through His eternal vision He will deliver just at the right time, we can have peace. One of the resources God has promised us is the power to live Godly lives. *As we know Jesus better, his divine power gives us everything we need for living a godly life. He has called us to receive his own glory and goodness!* (See 2 Peter 1:1-11) Because we cannot live Godly lives on our own, God allows us to share in his divine nature to help us to live a life that is free of sin. The more we work at practicing moral behavior the stronger our Christian character grows. As our Christian character grows, we get to know God better, we have better self-control, we develop more patient endurance, and we love others. These do not come automatically or easy but require hard, diligent work. They are not optional but God requires them of us. We do not have the luxury of perfecting one and then start on another but we must work on them all together. We can rest assured that God has given us the power we need to accomplish these changes in our lives but we have the responsibility to learn and to grow.

As Christians, God not only expects us to have peace within but also he expects us to promote peace with others. We must *work hard at living in peace with others*. Genesis, chapter 26 provides a good example. God blessed Isaac to acquire tremendous wealth. He harvested one hundred times more grain than he planted, he had large flocks of sheep and goats and many servants. His neighbors, the Philistines, who had been very friendly with Isaac, saw how God had blessed him and they became very jealous. Jealousy is a dividing force strong enough to tear apart mighty nations or the closest friends. The land where the two groups lived was located on the edge of the desert and so water was as precious as gold. Isaac and his servants dug a well that produced much water. The Philistines ruined the well by filling it in with dirt. Although this was considered an act of war during this period, Isaac and his servants moved to a different location. At the new location, the same thing happened again. Three times Isaac and his men dug new wells. When the first two disputes over the wells arose, Isaac moved on and left the land to the Philistines. Finally, there was enough room for everyone. Rather than engage in war with his adversary, Isaac compromised for the sake of peace. I can recall while growing up in my great grandmother's house my brother and I would sometimes fight over a toy or some other object. I was older and perhaps stronger so when my brother would cry, my grandmother would say, "For peace sake let him have it." Only recently did I come to understand what she meant. When we have God's spirit living within us, His influence in our lives will attract others—even our enemies. When this happens, we must take the opportunity to reach out to them with God's love.

In order for us to experience the peace of God, we must be in complete obedience to His word and remove everything that is not like God from our lives. We must also free ourselves of all the things that prevent us from committing ourselves wholeheartedly to serving God. *Remove the pagan altars and shrines. Smash the sacred pillars and cut down the Asherah poles.* (Please see 2 Chronicles 14:1-6) Going to church and doing good deeds is not enough. We must eliminate sinful practices from our lives. If we ask God continually to help up remove the sources of our temptation, He will help us. Soon, we will find we do not miss the nightclub, or the hip-hop music, or the alcohol, or the drugs, or the tobacco, or the pornography, or the homosexuality, or the fornication, or the adultery, or the gossip. In their place, we will find that God has given us the perfect peace of living in harmony with Him. The result of the Holy Spirit's work in our lives is a deep and lasting peace. Worldly peace is absence of conflict but God's peace is a confident assurance in any circumstance that all things work together for good for those who love God and are obedient to his word.

Patience

Longsuffering, endurance, forbearance, and the ability to accept that not everyone is as perfect as we are (sic) and therefore we allow him or her a mistake or two as they grow characterize this divine virtue or fruit of the Spirit.

Wait patiently for the Lord. Be brave and courageous. Yes, wait patiently for the Lord. (Please see Psalm 27:14) Samuel anointed David as king at age 16 but he did not become king until age 30. During the wait, a jealous King Saul chased him throughout the wilderness as he sought to kill him. Waiting on God is not always easy. Sometimes it appears he does not hear us at all or that he does not understand the urgency of our situation. *The Lord is my inheritance, therefore, I will hope in him! The Lord is wonderfully good to those who wait for him and seek him. So it is good to wait quietly for salvation from the Lord.* (Please see Lamentation 3:24-26) We can put our hope in and wait for God because he uses our waiting time to refresh, renew, and to teach us. We should make good use of our waiting time by discovering what God may be trying to teach us during that time.

Whenever trouble comes your way, let it be an opportunity for joy. When your faith is tested, your endurance has a chance to grow. So let it grow. When your endurance is fully developed, you will be strong in character and ready for anything. (Please see James 1:2-4) When—not if—troubles or difficulties come, we must see the opportunity to profit from them. We should not pretend to be happy about our trouble but have a positive outlook because of what the situation or circumstance can produce in our lives. Tough times can strengthen our endurance. Besides this, we cannot know the depth of our character until we see how we will react under pressure. It is easy to love and be kind to others when everything is going well in our lives. But can we still be kind to others when we are being treated unfairly or when there is trouble all around us? Instead of complaining about our troubles, we should see them as opportunities to grow. Each time we *go through* a difficult situation we *come out* more mature and more complete than before. Thank God for making us mature and complete and for promising to be with us through the tough times. Ask God to help you solve your problems or to give you the strength to endure them. Be patient. God will not leave you alone with your problems; he will stay close and help you grow. *God will give eternal life to those who persist in doing what is good, seeking after the glory and honor and immortality that God offers.* (Please see Romans 2:7)

Those who patiently and persistently do the will of God find eternal life. We are not saved by our good deeds, however when we commit our lives fully to God we want to please him and do his will. Good deeds are a grateful response to what God has done, not a prerequisite to earning his favor. *We can rejoice, too, when we run into problems and trials, for we know that they are good for us—they help us learn to endure. And endurance develops strength of character in us, and character strengthens our confident expectation of salvation. And this expectation will not disappoint us. For we know clearly God loves us, because he has given us the Holy Spirit to fill our hearts with his love.* (Please see Roman 5:3-5) Our problems strengthen our trust in God and give us greater confidence about the future. Each time we emerge from a difficult situation, it becomes one we can look back on and remember how God brought us through it. When we face the next challenge, we are confident that we will be victorious because of having faced similar challenges in the past.

It is through this same process the Spirit helps to free us from our addictions. Each "little" success in resisting the world's temptations builds on the previous one to strengthen our faith that God will deliver us from our habits. When God saves us, He also takes away all unrighteousness. It does not all happen at once, so we begin to see that we are gradually dropping all the "little" bad habits that have controlled us for years. Each time we have overcome one of these little monsters, we must thank God for removing it. When we have done this, the Holy Spirit will give us the strength to overcome the next one.

We try to live in such a way that no one will be hindered from finding the Lord by the way we act, and so no one can find fault with our ministry. In everything we do, we try to show that we are true ministers of God. We patiently endure troubles, hardships, and calamities of every kind. We have been beaten, been put in jail, faced angry mobs, worked to exhaustion, endured sleepless nights, and gone without food. We have proved ourselves by our purity, our understanding, our patience, our kindness, our sincere love, and the power of the Holy Spirit. (Please see 2 Corinthians 6:3-6)

As we know Jesus better, his divine power gives us everything we need for living a godly life. He has called us to receive his own glory and goodness. And by that same mighty power, he has given us all of his rich and wonderful promises. He has promised that we will escape the decadence all around us caused by evil desires and that you will share in his divine nature. So make every effort to apply the benefits of these promises to your life. Then your faith will produce a life of moral excellence. A life of moral excellence leads to knowing God better. Knowing God better leads to self-control. Self-control leads to patient endurance, and patient endurance leads to godliness. Godliness leads to love for other Christians, and finally you will grow to have genuine love for everyone. The more you grow like this, the more you will become productive and useful in your knowledge of our Lord Jesus Christ. (Please see 2 Peter 1:3-8)

Temptation comes from evil desires inside us, not from God. It begins with an evil thought and becomes sin when we dwell on the thought and allow it to become an action. Like a snowball rolling downhill, sin grows more destructive the more we let it have its way. The best time to stop a temptation is before it is too strong or moving too fast to control. God blesses those who patiently endure the testing.

The Holy Spirit produces in us the ability to exercise self-control in situations where the words or actions of others challenge us. Think of times when you listened to the Sunday school teacher attempt to teach when it was painfully obvious he was not prepared or when you heard the choir attempt to sing a song they had not rehearsed. Think of the time when someone said things to you in an attempt to insult you. Our carnal mind produces the desire to say bad things about the person who performs poorly or to retaliate against a person who hurls insults, but the Spirit produces the patience that allows us to bring our thoughts under control before we speak.

Goodness

. . . the beneficial qualities of something; kindness; morally right.

. . . I really want to do what is right, but I don't do it. Instead, I do the very thing I hate. I know perfectly well that what I am doing is wrong . . . But I can't help myself, because it is sin inside me that makes me do these evil things. No matter which way I turn, I can't make myself do right. I want to, but I can't. When I want to do what is good, I don't. And when I try not to do wrong, I do wrong anyway. It seems to be a fact of life that when I want to do what is right, I inevitably do what is wrong. I love God's law with all my heart. But there is another law at work within me that is at war with my mind. This other law wins the fight and makes me a slave to the sin that is still within me. Oh, what a miserable person I am! Who will free me from this life that is dominated by sin? Thank God! The answer is in Jesus Christ our Lord. (Please see Romans 7:15-25)

We are what our heart says we are. A good person produces good works from a good heart. But we are powerless to do this on our own. A heart transplant requires a heart surgeon. It is only by having the Holy Spirit living within us that we can have a good heart. The Holy Spirit will fill our hearts with new attitudes and new motives. *Make the tree good and the fruit will be good.*

We must be willing to make ourselves living sacrifices for God. In order to become living examples of God's goodness we must esteem others more important than ourselves. Therefore, we must not pretend to love others or just say we love but really love them so they know we love them.

I read today of a young mother who was arrested for the death of her two small children. It appears that her baby sitter canceled just before the young mother was to report to her job. She took the two small children in the car with a battery powered fan, food and water, and drove to work. She left the young children in the car while she worked eight hours of a scheduled 16-hour shift before telling her supervisor she could stay no longer. She found the children unconscious but alive and she took them home instead of to a hospital. Police found her at her small apartment wailing and screaming over the two dead toddlers. I immediately thought, "Someone failed her." Someone should have loved her enough that she felt safe in leaving her children with them while she worked. Someone should have loved her enough that she felt safe enough to stay home from work, even if it meant losing her job. This was obviously an act of fear—afraid of losing the job or afraid to leave her children with someone else. As Christians, we have the power to love the fear out of others. We have the love of God within us and it is our responsibility to share that love with others. We must make others so comfortable in our love that they can feel assured that regardless of their current circumstances and whatever the present situation they are facing, they are not alone.

We must delight in honoring each other. We should not be lazy in our work but serve God with enthusiasm. When we see brothers and sisters in need, we should be the ones to help them. We should invite others to be guests in our homes for dinner and welcome those who need a place to spend the night. When our brothers and sisters are happy, we should be happy with them. When they are sad, we should share in their sorrow. We should not retaliate against those who persecute us because we are Christians but pray God's blessings for them. We must do all that is within our power to live in harmony with others. Do not discriminate against others by acting as if we are better than they are. Enjoy the company of ordinary people. We must not think that we know it all. Remember that good conquers evil. God approves of those who are good, but he condemns those who plan wickedness.

Kindness

. . . benevolent; gentle

You are to be perfect, even as your Father in heaven is perfect. This is a "tough saying." But Jesus said it. See Matthew 5:48. Therefore, we strive for perfection in four areas: (1) In *character*—we want to be as much like Christ as possible. We might not be able to live a flawless life but we spend every day trying. (2) In *holiness*—we must separate ourselves from the sinful values the world holds, devote ourselves to fulfilling God's desires for our lives and spread His love and mercy into the world. (3) In *maturity*—we do not achieve Christ-like character overnight but we grow more and more like him every day. We grow by practicing those behaviors he has taught us, such as showing kindness to those who hate us. (4) In *love*—we must strive to love others completely just as God loves us.

There was a believer in Joppa named Tabitha. She was always doing kind things for others and helping the poor. (Please see Acts 9:36) What a way to be remembered! This lady made an impact on the community in which she lived by doing kind things for others. We too can make an impact on the communities where we live. When we show kindness to others, they are more likely to show kindness to someone else. In this way, we spread kindness into the world.

Since God has chosen us to be the holy people whom he loves, we must clothe ourselves with tenderhearted mercy, kindness, humility, gentleness, and patience. (Please see Colossians 3:12) When we are kind to each other, from a tender heart, with a forgiving attitude, we can love out the bitterness, rage, anger, harsh words, slander and all types of malicious behavior. Not only do we love it out of the other person but also we love it out of ourselves.

Faithfulness

. . . firm in adherence; utterly loyal

When Abram was ninety-nine years old, the Lord appeared to him and said, "I am God Almighty; serve me faithfully and live a blameless life. I will make a covenant with you, by which I will guarantee to make you into a mighty nation." (Please see Genesis 17:1-2) What a promise to make to a 99-year old man! What a God who is powerful enough to deliver! What a reason to be faithful! In order to serve God faithfully, we must do all the things that His Word, the bible, tells us to do.

If we are faithful to the end, trusting God as firmly as when we first believed, we will share in all that belongs to Christ. (Please see Hebrews 4:14)

Faithfulness has rewards. *Remain faithful even when facing death and I will give you the crown of life.* (Please see Revelation 2:10) We must remain faithful even during troubles and times of suffering, remembering that God is in control and his promises are reliable and true.

So the Lord gave to Israel all the land he had sworn to give their ancestors, and they conquered it and settled there. And the Lord gave them rest on every side, just as he had solemnly promised their ancestors. None of their enemies could stand against them, for the Lord helped them conquer all their enemies. All of the good promises that the Lord had given Israel came true. (Please see Joshua 21:43-45) God proved faithful in fulfilling every promise he had given to Israel. Fulfillment of some promises took many years, but "all of the good promises that the Lord had given Israel came true." He fulfils His promises according to His timetable, not ours, but we know that his word is sure. The more we learn of those promises God has fulfilled and continues to fulfill, the easier it is to hope for those yet to come. Sometimes we become impatient, wanting God to act in a certain way right now. Instead, we should faithfully do what we know he wants us to do and trust him for the future.

Since we know that God is faithful and we know that God wants us to live a righteous and holy life, we have confidence that he will help us to do what is right. We should remain faithful to Him just as He is faithful to us. And if our heart's desire is to be free of sin and to effect a change in our lifestyle or to be free of bad habits or addictions, we must ask Him to help us, and the Holy Spirit will give us the power to overcome these obstacles.

God's word, through 2 Peter 1:5, offers this promise: *As we know Jesus better, his divine power gives us everything we need for living a godly life. He has called us to receive his own glory and goodness! And by that same power he has given us all of his rich and wonderful promises. He has promised that you will escape the decadence all around you caused by evil desires and the your will share in his divine nature.* Amen!

The Role of Fasting

The gospel writers record that Jesus healed a demon-possessed boy. His disciples had attempted to heal the boy, but they were unable to cast out the demon. After Jesus had commanded the demon to leave the child, the disciples asked, "Master, why could we not cast it out?" Jesus replied, "This kind can come out only by prayer and fasting." *(See Mark 9:29) **

If you have a demon or a bad habit that you are finding extremely difficult to break, I recommend prayer and fasting. I have not said, "I recommend fasting." Much prayer must accompany your fasting. If your goal is to change a particular area in your life, you must determine in your heart that you are going to exorcise the demon and continually pray to God for strength and for the help of the Holy Spirit. In addition to a deep spiritual commitment and faith in God, you should also know something of the medical and physiological characteristic of the habit you are trying to break. Where there are strong relationships between two or more additions, it may be necessary to give up both simultaneously. I found it helpful to give up alcohol and tobacco at the same time. So, talk to your doctor and pray for the help of the Holy Spirit. What follows are little lessons learned from my own experience.

The carnal mind says, "Make an exception today because it is the weekend." I have made it through the week eating nothing between sunrise and sunset and at night eating only bread, fruits and vegetables and drinking only water, except for one cup of black or green tea with half teaspoon of sugar in the early morning for cleansing. I am attempting to fast this way for 40 days. There are several reasons for attempting this fast. I am praying that God will help me to bring my physical body into complete submission to my spirit. There are still too many things in my life with the potential to control me; if not completely, they could severely restrict my spiritual progress. I eat too much fat because of my love for fried foods and meats smothered in gravy. My physical body loves soft drinks, especially cola, and it loves ice cream. I consume much too much of both. I sleep an average of four hours each night and even that is with interruption. I have this constant desire for sexual intimacy. Satan knows my weaknesses. Because he does, there is opportunity to exploit those weaknesses to interrupt my prayer life, to take my focus off maintaining my relationship with God, to cause me to commit spiritual adultery and even place my wife's wishes over God. I am praying that God will give me a deeper inner strength through His precious Holy Spirit. I want Jesus to become more and more at home in my heart and for me to become more and more like Him in my everyday life. It is my desire to have so strong a faith and trust in God that whenever temptation confronts me, the Holy Spirit will speak to me in scriptures just as He did Jesus in the wilderness. In addition to these things, through the grace and mercy of God, I want to present my body a living sacrifice, holy and acceptable to God. I want to live in such a way that my words and actions bring glory to His name. I pray that through the fast God will help me to develop the strength and endurance necessary to make Him my focus in every work.

So on this Saturday morning my carnal mind says I should celebrate and have another cup of tea. However, I have been here before. This is why the scripture says we should count in all joy when we face trials in our life. They become the experiences of the past that enable us to deal effectively with the struggles that lie ahead of us. As I struggled to free myself from the chains of alcohol and tobacco, my mind would often tell me I should celebrate having reached a milestone by having a small drink or smoking a cigar. But thanks to Almighty God, the Holy Spirit empowered me to resist and to understand this trick of the evil one. Little compromises like these cause us to go through a constant cycle of starting over again. Instead of reaching the "promised land" and achieving the freedom God has given us and Jesus gave his life for, we go round and round in the wilderness until we become dead.

One day I slept later than usual. Except for our youngest daughter, who is classic "early to bed and early to rise," the others in the house expect me to awake them. So we are all late. Instead of making breakfast for myself, I helped my son to get his things together so he would not miss the school bus. With that done, I showered, dressed, and was ready to go and the sun had not risen. On my way out the door, I grabbed a banana, a pack of crackers, and a glass of water. I thought to myself, "I can still eat these before sunrise." Once outside, I noticed the ice on the cars was thick and hard. I started the engine in my truck and began to scrape through the ice. As I was doing this, I remembered seeing our daughter scurrying about as I was preparing to leave. So, I went inside to see if she needed anything from me for the day before she went of to her classes at a local college. She said she was fine and that she would be leaving in just a minute or two. Immediately I thought to myself, "It will take you at least five minutes to get the ice off your car." So with the scraper in my hand, I went out and removed the ice from her car. As I jumped in the truck to leave, I saw the sun peeping over the horizon. I looked over at the banana and crackers. My carnal mind said, "It's okay just this one time because you were trying to do a good thing for someone else." Then the spiritual mind said, "Your commitment was to not take any food from sunrise to sunset. If you compromise here then it's over. You can break your commitment now or you can trust God that you will make it through the day without food."

A co-worker had trouble with her car that day, and after work I drove her first to her mother's house and then dropped her off at her home. After that, I picked up some things at the store for my wife. As I am driving home in the dark and feeling very hungry, I noticed the banana and crackers in a box between the seats and immediately thought, "Oh how wonderful it is to have a God who sees into our future and prepares the way for us while we are completely unaware." My hunger left.

Romans 8:
Life in the Spirit

So now there is no condemnation for those who belong to Christ Jesus. And because you belong to him, the power of the life-giving Spirit has freed you from the power of sin that leads to death. The Law of Moses was unable to save us because of the weakness of our sinful nature. So God did what the law could not do. He sent his own Son in a body like the bodies we sinners have. And in that body God declared an end to sin's control over us by giving his Son as a sacrifice for our sins. He did this so that the just requirement of the law would be fully satisfied for us, who no longer follow our sinful nature but instead follow the Spirit.

Those who are dominated by the sinful nature think about sinful things, but those who are controlled by the Holy Spirit think about things that please the Spirit. So letting your sinful nature control your mind leads to death. But letting the Spirit control your mind leads to life and peace. For the sinful nature is always hostile to God. It never did obey God's laws, and it never will. That is why those who are still under the control of their sinful nature can never please God.

But you are not controlled by your sinful nature. You are controlled by the Spirit if you have the Spirit of God living in you. (And remember that those who do not have the Spirit of Christ living in them do not belong to him at all.) And Christ lives within you, so even though your body will die because of sin, the Spirit gives you life because you have been made right with God. The Spirit of God, who raised Jesus from the dead, lives in you. And just as God raised Christ Jesus from the dead, he will give life to your mortal bodies by this same Spirit living within you.

Therefore, dear brothers and sisters, you have no obligation to do what your sinful nature urges you to do. If you live by its dictates, you will die. But if through the power of the Spirit you put to death the deeds of your sinful nature, you will live. For all who are led by the Spirit of God are children of God.

Ephesians 5:
Living in the Light

Imitate God, therefore, in everything you do, because you are his dear children. Live a life filled with love, following the example of Christ. He loved us and offered himself as a sacrifice for us, a pleasing aroma to God.

Let there be no sexual immorality, impurity, or greed among you. Such sins have no place among God's people. Obscene stories, foolish talk, and coarse jokes—these are not for you. Instead, let there be thankfulness to God. You can be sure that no immoral, impure, or greedy person will inherit the Kingdom of Christ and of God. For a greedy person is an idolater, worshiping the things of this world.

Do not be fooled by those who try to excuse these sins, for the anger of God will fall on all who disobey him. Do not participate in the things these people do. Once you were full of darkness, but now you have light from the Lord. So live as people of light! For this light within you produces only what is good, right, and true.

Carefully determine what pleases the Lord. Take no part in the worthless deeds of evil and darkness; instead, expose them. It is shameful even to talk about the things that ungodly people do in secret. But their evil intentions will be exposed when the light shines on them, for the light makes everything visible. This is why the scripture says, "Awake, O sleeper, rise up from the dead, and Christ will give you light."

Colossians 3: Living the New Life

Since you have been raised to new life with Christ, set your sights on the realities of heaven, where Christ sits in the place of honor at God's right hand. Think about the things of heaven, not the things of earth. For you died to this life, and your real life is hidden with Christ in God. And when Christ, who is your life, is revealed to the whole world, you will share in all his glory.

So put to death the sinful, earthly things lurking within you. Have nothing to do with sexual immorality, impurity, lust, and evil desires. Do not be greedy, for a greedy person is an idolater, worshiping the things of this world. Because of these sins, the anger of God is coming. You used to do these things when your life was still part of this world. Now is the time to get rid of anger, rage, malicious behavior, slander, and dirty language. Do not lie to each other, for you have stripped off your old sinful nature and all its wicked deeds. Put on your new nature, and be renewed as you learn to know your Creator and become like him. In this new life, it does not matter if you are a Jew or a Gentile, circumcised or uncircumcised, barbaric, uncivilized, slave, or free. Christ is all that matters and he lives in all of us.

Since God chose you to be the holy people he loves, you must clothe yourselves with tenderhearted mercy, kindness, humility, gentleness, and patience. Make allowance for each other's faults, and forgive anyone who offends you. Remember, the Lord forgave you, so you must forgive others. Above all, clothe yourselves with love, which binds us all together in perfect harmony. And let the peace that comes from Christ rule in your hearts. For as members of one body you are called to live in peace. And always be thankful.

Let the message about Christ, in all its richness, fill your lives. Teach and counsel each other with all the wisdom he gives. Sing psalms, hymns, and spiritual songs to God with thankful hearts. And whatever you do or say, do it as a representative of the Lord Jesus, giving thanks through him to God the Father.

Living by the Spirit's Power

We must be careful how we live. If we live our lives any way we desire, without considering the consequences our actions will have on others as well as ourselves, we live as fools. We must make the most of every opportunity to learn how God, the creator and giver of life, desires for us to live. We must not be drunk with alcohol, drugs, sexual desires, greed, envy, jealousy, or any other thing that clouds our thinking and take control of our lives. These things all lead to ruin. Instead, we should pray and ask God to fill us with His Holy Spirit. The same God who gives salvation will also remove all unrighteousness (sin) from our lives. If you ask Him with all sincerity, not many days will pass before you begin to experience a change in your heart, in your thoughts, and in your actions. You will begin to understand from the scriptures how God wants you to live. You will begin to see and understand the terrible influence some people and some places have had on you, and you will no longer have the desire to visit them. You will begin to be in a relationship with God that allows continual prayer and fellowship. He becomes available, through the Spirit and through Jesus Christ the intercessor, for minute-by-minute consultations. You will be able to feel His presence all through the day as He gives you whatever you need through the power of the Holy Spirit.

In order to make our bodies a living sacrifice, holy and acceptable unto God and to be ready for any good work to which He calls us, we must bring our minds and our bodies into complete submission to our spirit. If we have determined to do this, the Holy Spirit is our helper. Without him, we can do nothing. We can do all things through Christ Jesus who strengthens us.

I pray that reading this book has blessed you and that you will not neglect to study God's word to learn what it is He wants you to do. I pray He will give you the strength to overcome all obstacles to living a life of complete freedom in the Spirit.